THE
ARTISANAL
HOME

To our grandparents

THE ARTISANAL HOME

Interiors and Furniture of Casamidy

Jorge Almada and Anne-Marie Midy

with Ingrid Abramovitch
Preface by Anita Sarsidi
Foreword by Celerie Kemble

RIZZOLI
NEW YORK

New York · Paris · London · Milan

CONTENTS

PREFACE

FOREWORD

Anne-Marie Midy and Jorge Almada are obsessed with the "palpable." By that I mean that my longtime friends, founders of the design firm Casamidy, are drawn to making, collecting, and extolling the handmade—expressed in objects and interiors where the human hand is in constant evidence. Chairs are dressed with fabrics that have been laboriously loomed strand by strand. A metal table declares its workshop origins—from the delicate soldering that marries its elements to the lustrous sheen that can only be achieved through patient rubbing by hand—while a tin headboard has been carefully stamped with symmetrical patterns. Finishes are often timeworn, and floors are frequently spread with woven-fiber mats—the kind of natural textiles that crunch underfoot, their sound adding yet another layer of atmosphere. Put these all together and you get the rooms that Casamidy has become known for—hauntingly beautiful spaces that breathe, that commune, that comfort.

—Anita Sarsidi

My first impression of Anne-Marie Midy and Jorge Almada arrived in the form of a beautiful little folded map that was sent to my office about ten years ago. Unfolded, the map revealed photographs of Casamidy's most recent collection of handmade home accessories and furniture, set on brightly colored squares and speaking volumes, it seemed to me, about a very fabulous and authentic life being lived by a young couple in San Miguel de Allende.

As someone busy trying to build her own fabulous, authentic life (and business) in New York City, I was intrigued. Here were highly luxurious, artisanal pieces that combined a deep respect for tradition with a very sophisticated contemporary sensibility and the highest quality craftsmanship. Looking at them, I had the surreal experience of not knowing Anne-Marie and Jorge at all, yet feeling I caught the scent of many of the things I cared about most in their work. It was like peeking though a tiny bougainvillea-draped window and glimpsing a marvelous world inside—one in which soul and sophistication, nostalgia and modernity, luxury and authenticity and integrity all came together in service of an aesthetic that was both deeply familiar and not quite like

The rug in the library of our Brussels home was custom-made in Tibet. Whenever possible I like to commission designs from indigenous communities as I am always so inspired by their cultural heritage and artisanal knowledge. The carpet's checkerboard pattern was chosen to balance the room's many curvaceous elements, including the furnishings and the marble fireplace. Our "Ixelles" bench is covered in an ikat silk; the "Symi" armchair is upholstered in velvet and has a Belgian-linen back cushion.

anything I'd ever seen before. I started placing orders immediately.

Since then I've come to know more about Anne-Marie and Jorge, through the process of working with them on many interior design projects in which I've used their furniture for clients in a range of settings—from Virginia to L.A., Texas to the Hamptons. I often seek the expressiveness of their pieces, the handmade mastery of their metal and leather crafters. I've watched their business evolve with great respect and have enjoyed a growing sense of professional interdependency with them and the craftspeople they employ.

When my husband and I began building our own family compound in the Dominican Republic several years ago, I knew I wanted Casamidy included in what I think of as our foundational furniture because of the inherent character (or "thumbprint," as Jorge calls it) of the workshops in San Miguel. Their furniture has soul. It's made right and you can feel that.

With their book layouts in my hands, I've finally had the chance to go inside and explore the glorious world of Jorge and Anne-Marie that I imagined so many years ago. And what a world it is! From their townhouse in Brussels with its delicious violet library to their Parisian jewel-box flat on the Rue de Condé, from Anne-Marie's charming family villa in Saint-Paul-de-Vence to their magnificent rooftop garden overlooking San Miguel, Jorge and Anne-Marie have created a truly enchanted universe for themselves. Looking through the pages, you can't help but think: man, these people know how to live.

As someone with her own passion for beloved old family homes, the question of how to honor the history of these places while instilling a fresh and lively sense of the present is a constant one for me. Anne-Marie and Jorge are masters of this particular challenge. They know exactly when to respect something old for being perfect, how to pitch it when it's cliché, and how to mix it all in beautifully with their own designs. From their custom-made Tibetan rugs in Paris to the showstopping green malachite window shades in Belgium, from the ultramodern crunched Aldo Chaparro aluminum sculpture above the mantel to the pre-Columbian artifacts on the Casamidy "Collier" table, their sensibility is so vibrant and original, so engaged in creating a constant, witty, and thoughtful dialogue between past and present that it is clear Casamidy could only be achieved jointly and as a culmination of generations of design appreciation. This book is intimate. It shows how much love is in their designs, and in and for their homes.

It is an honor to be invited into Anne-Marie and Jorge's world through these pages. It is the sort of gracious, welcoming place we all dream of—one where you can imagine being told to kick off your shoes and wander up to the terrace for a bite of cheese, lots of wine, and a chance to appreciate a beautiful life.

—Celerie Kemble

A collection of objects that have personal meaning: an oil painting by Anne Pesce, my mother's ostrich eggs, miniature tin racing cars, and a postcard sketch by a friend. I like to combine different shapes and materials to create a still life like the one on this marble mantel.

PART ONE
ARTISANAL HOMES AND
FURNISHINGS

INTRODUCTION

My name is Jorge Almada. My partner both in life and in work is Anne-Marie Midy. Together, we founded our design firm Casamidy in 1998. We created this book together as well, but, as with everything we do, there was a division of labor. In order to maintain the integrity of our voices, I wrote this introduction and the chapter texts. Anne-Marie, a trained graphic designer, executed the book's layouts. She also wrote all the photograph captions. This book reflects our collective vision.

Anne-Marie and I met in New York in 1994 when she was working as an art director at *Martha Stewart Living* magazine and I was a student at Parsons School of Design in Greenwich Village. We discovered that we had much in common, even though I am from Mexico and she is from France. Though we had lived continents apart, we both had learned at a young age to appreciate the pleasures of an artfully appointed home. We discovered that we had each spent a great deal of time when we were growing up with our grandparents, who played an important role in shaping our idea of what is essential in making a home not only functional but also visually interesting.

Both our French and Mexican grandparents had spent a lifetime creating living spaces that were elegant and deeply personal. Their homes were filled with antiques and artisanal pieces.

They worked hand in hand with local artisans. To be sure, the decorating style of that time was a great deal more formal than the way we live today. Nevertheless, our grandparents' houses, furnished with unique and handcrafted pieces, have been a major source of inspiration for both Anne-Marie and me.

My ancestors were originally from Alamos in the Mexican state of Sonora. The family later moved to the fertile valley of Culiacán in northern Mexico to start a sugar refinery. There, my great-grandparents built a rather austere *casona*, a Spanish Colonial–style townhouse. In 1928, my grandmother Alicia—the daughter of Plutarco Elías Calles, a revolutionary general who became the president of Mexico—married my grandfather, who was also named Jorge Almada. They remodeled the *casona* in the 1940s, adding such modern touches as a courtyard pool and tiled corridors. In the 1950s, they had an Airstream trailer that they outfitted as a bar. They would travel with it to friends' isolated ranches and to the beach.

The first ten years of my life were spent at the house in Culiacán and I have fond memories of roller-skating there with my sister, Natalia, in the grand hallway with its geometric-patterned floors. My father had a small plane and we would sometimes fly to our farm near the coast or visit our small ranch, El Bellotal, in the

preceding spread A room in the crumbling, largely nineteenth-century hacienda Jaral de Berrio, which is located near San Miguel—a place of inspiration where we have frequently photographed our Casamidy creations. Our "Symi" chair, wrapped in leather straps, looks at home in this hauntingly beautiful space.

opposite Our "Branch" table in a gold-leaf finish mimics the huisache shrubs that cover the San Miguel countryside. Pre-Columbian pottery has been placed on the glass surface.

above and right Jorge and I like to mix the past with the present. His grandfather designed the table, which is surrounded by eight "Grenadier" armchairs in the dining area at Hospicio, our townhouse in San Miguel. It was necessary to make the table narrower to fit the space. The black-and-white photograph dating from the 1940s shows the same table in the family house in Culiacán, Mexico.

opposite The Culiacán house was built in 1882 in the Colonial style, with a spacious entry hall and hand-carved ebony columns. The cement floor tiles date from the 1950s.

Sierra Mountains of the state of Sonora. My parents later relocated the family to Phoenix, Arizona, where we crammed all of the family furniture into a small southwestern-style house. My parents later divorced and my dad returned to Mexico City, where he wedged the same furniture into a succession of modest apartments (my mother, Lynn, also returned to Mexico and now lives on the coast near Puerto Vallarta). I sometimes think that my desire to become a furniture designer stems from a belief that furniture seemingly endures, even when everything else is in perpetual flux.

For Anne-Marie, her beloved grandmother Monique Manchez Midy was a mentor. She was a woman who brimmed with artistic talent and approached everything she did with passion. She loved to create faux decorative finishes and would roll up her sleeves to hand-paint a shifting blue sky in the vestibule of her Paris apartment. She surrounded herself with beauty—from the decor of her Paris apartment and the renovation of her stone farmhouse in Normandy to the gardens she created at her home in Saint-Paul-de-Vence. She encouraged Anne-Marie in her desire to become an artist and was pleased when her granddaughter enrolled in the Rhode Island School of Design, where she studied graphic design.

Monique passed away in France in 1996. Shortly afterwards Anne-Marie's father sold La Belle Angerie, his mother's manor house in Normandy. Anne-Marie and I flew to France and took the train from Paris to Caen to say good-bye to the house. It was set in a landscape of rolling farmland located directly behind Sword Beach, the code name given to one of the main areas where the British landed on

D-Day. I later learned that Monique had been involved in the French Resistance and that she had chosen to build her house on this location in remembrance of the dramatic events she had lived through. The property consisted of an immense stone barn that she used as her painting studio, a round *colombier* (pigeon house), and a rustic farmhouse filled with beautiful furnishings. During her childhood Anne-Marie had spent many happy times with her grandmother here. She had visited the windswept Normandy beaches, biked through the surrounding countryside, and sunbathed in her grandmother's flower gardens when the weather permitted.

Two years before Anne-Marie and I founded Casamidy, we visited the Hermès workshops in Pantin, France. The ateliers were located in a central atrium with lots of sunlight. Blue-smocked artisans, completely immersed in their projects, were working on floors designated to their particular skill sets: silk-screening, ironwork, leatherwork, and so on. As we peered down the metal catwalks, I realized that Mexico, a country filled with traditional artisans, would be an ideal place to develop a unique line of handmade home accessories.

Upon returning to New York, I set off to Mexico in hopes of finding talented craftspeople and sourcing local materials. Realizing that Anne-Marie and I couldn't collaborate on this venture long-distance, I asked her to join me in Mexico City. She then quit her job at *Martha Stewart Living* and I promptly received a very concerned phone call from her father. I tried to convince him that living in Mexico would give Anne-Marie the creative freedom she needed and that ultimately it would be good for her career. He turned out to be actually quite open-minded about this prospect, having himself spent time in Mexico as a bachelor in the 1960s.

The first Casamidy collection was inspired by indigenous Mexican *artesanía*. We collaborated with Marta Turok, an anthropologist who had reintroduced natural dyes and dyeing techniques to indigenous weavers throughout Mexico. This experience exposed us to the extraordinary range of Mexican textiles. We put together a collection of accessories based on such traditional Mexican items as hand-lacquered *maques* (gourds), henequen fiber boxes, cast-aluminum trays, wax candles that

opposite My childhood apartment in Paris (top). The *colombier* (pigeon house) at the end of the cobblestone road at my grandmother's home, La Belle Angerie, in a small town in Normandy, France (bottom).

above La Belle Angerie used to be a working farm. The *abreuvoir* (drinking trough) was converted into a pond, located between the guesthouse and my grandmother's studio.

resembled fruit, woven straw animals, copper plates, and more. The inaugural Casamidy catalog had bright squares delineating each project and was folded like a map. For our first show at Paris's international trade fair Maison et Objet, we placed these colorful maps in traditional Mexican *mercado* (market) bags and handed them out. They were snatched up faster than hot bread, or *pan caliente*, as we say in Mexico.

In 1999, growing tired of the congestion of Mexico City, Anne-Marie and I moved to San Miguel de Allende, a small colonial town in the central Mexican highlands. Anne-Marie and I had been working with tinsmiths in San Miguel and decided that the picturesque town would make a logical base for designing and manufacturing our products. In 2002, Anne-Marie received her first interior design job: the renovation of a Colonial-style house on San Miguel's Sollano Street. In working on the project, she was having a difficult time finding appropriate furniture beyond what she could glean in local antiques shops.

Up until then, we had always scoffed at the idea of using wrought iron for our designs. We associated the material with old-fashioned patio furniture. But we soon started noticing the beautiful iron railings and balustrades that you can find throughout San Miguel. As it turns out, one of the best blacksmiths in town, Refugio Garcia, happened to be our amicable next-door neighbor. Anne-Marie began a working relationship with Refugio when she commissioned him to make a large sofa based on the ornate styling of Colonial window grills.

Refugio's tiny workshop was rudimentary—just a small room that housed an anvil, a bellow, a collection of hammers, and a soldering iron. In the corner of his work space Anne-Marie spotted a group of square wrought-iron rods. It sparked an idea and, for the next two days, she feverishly sketched a series of life-size scaled silhouettes on kraft paper of what would become one of Casamidy's best sellers, the Varenne "Opera" chair. The design referenced a pair of classic eighteenth-century Louis XVI chairs that belonged to her mother, Marilyn. Anne-Marie perfected the curves and after about ten days the Casamidy medallion-backed iron-framed chair was born. We tested the prototype on our living room floor. This chair became a successful product for Casamidy—it inspired a new creative direction for our firm, which has since grown to encompass a comprehensive furniture line. Today, Casamidy employs sixty master artisans and a studio staff of four full-time employees. We relish the challenges of designing from scratch in collaboration with these talented individuals.

The homes featured in this book express our commitment to design that is completely made by hand. Whether it's a curtain that has been hand embroidered, a wall finish that has been painstakingly applied by a master plasterer, or an iron table hammered by a skilled blacksmith, an object that has the thumbprint of the artisan has an expressiveness that cannot be replicated by machine-made products. And like our grandparents, we believe that a home is a perpetual work in progress. We are constantly referencing the past, while at the same time always trying to stay open to new ideas.

above and left A 1964 photograph of my grandmother, an important figure in my life, with my father in her studio at La Belle Angerie. They are seated in Louis XIII–style chairs, which are now in a guest room in our Brussels home.

following spread The smooth lacquered surface of the "Condé" desk makes sketching a pleasure. The "Selle" chair easily slips under the desk to clear the passageway. I hung a steel cord from the floor lamp—this is where I keep inspirational pictures, wallpaper swatches, and clippings secured in place with magnets.

HOME WORK SPACES

Home offices are highly personal. At home in Brussels, we are lucky to have enough space for separate work spaces for Anne-Marie and me. We planned the design of these spaces to suit our individual needs.

My studio, located near the attic, has a slanted roof and a skylight that provides diffused natural light. I rarely need to turn on the lights in the room until evening. I use a leather-top desk with no drawers. I had my desk custom fitted with a top in thick saddle leather, which feels great to the touch (never too hot or cold) and eliminates the need for a mouse pad. I try to keep my work surface uncluttered, sticking to my basic tools of the trade: sketchbooks, a pair of cups filled with pencils, and a large wooden clothespin that I use for pinning papers.

As a designer, much time is spent daydreaming. This is why in my office I also have two modular B&B Italia leather sofas from the 1980s. They are very comfortable to lie down on. As the room is also my personal retreat, I furnished it

above Jorge's office is located on the top floor of our Brussels townhouse. He calls it his man cave; I refer to it as his bubble. Set away from the noise of daily living, this is a peaceful enclave. Sunlight streams through the skylight. A pair of "Almidi" raw metal bookshelves take over one side of the room.

opposite Displayed on the shelves are such meaningful objects as his father's Gucci leather briefcase and his vintage airplane collection. Passionate about leather, Jorge's desktop is clad in this material as are the two modular B&B Italia sofas that he sometimes uses as a daybed. Our border terrier makes himself at home here. A Charlotte Perriand "Courchevel" leather-and-chrome side chair from the 1970s that we found in Brussels is against the wall.

with family photos and objects that I collect, including leather boxes and airplane-related paraphernalia and models. My prized possession is a lithograph of a Spitfire signed by the Battle of Britain pilots, including Brian Kingcome, who was a squadron leader and, by coincidence, a manufacturer of sofas after World War II.

Anne-Marie's home office is located in a large converted bedroom on the third floor of our Brussels townhouse. It is situated just down the hall from our boys' shared bedroom, close enough for Anne-Marie to keep her maternal antennae out even as she works. In the evening, she'll hear it if one of our sons decides to get out of bed and roam around.

For the wall color, Anne-Marie selected a rich oxblood, which creates a feeling of intimacy in the space. Another advantage of this room is that it has north light—an indirect source of natural illumination, which is highly prized by artists for its constancy—streaming in through large windows. She is a hunter and gatherer of inspiration and her office is layered with the references—magazine clippings, photos, and postcards—that she refers to on a daily basis. She displays them on the marble mantelpiece or pins them onto a bulletin board. The office is furnished with a portable Belgian army desk (its many cubbyholes are convenient for organizing personal items and work-related papers) and a dining table that serves as her primary work surface. Meanwhile, the room's shelving is crammed with Anne-Marie's numerous books and magazines, not to mention the elaborate Lego structures that our boys love to create.

above My office may seem untidy but as a multitasking mother I know where everything—from Métro tickets to fabric swatches—is located. Clockwise from top left: I surround myself with objects that inspire me, from a clay donkey laden with miniature wax fruit to a small iron rooster. A 1950s black-and-white postcard collection—a souvenir from Nice—functions as the backdrop. Chinese binding shoes, my boys' Lego creations, a photograph of my great-grandfather with me, a friend's ink drawing, my grandfather's leather-cased clock, a hand-blown Venetian glass candy, an Hermès gold-star-studded agenda from the 1930s that belonged to my grandmother, and a heart-shaped Mexican *milagro*—these are some of the many items that clutter my space and make me feel at home.

opposite Since the room faces north, I warmed it up by painting the walls Farrow & Ball Blazer Red. My friend Paulo Netto took the colorful photograph of this Tibetan temple—the eye-catching perspective intrigues me. The 1950s portable Belgian army desk is perfect for organizing my papers and travel keepsakes.

PART TWO
INTERIORS

BRUSSELS

A TOWNHOUSE
in Brussels

If you would have told us a decade ago that we would one day move across the ocean from Mexico to Brussels, we might not have believed you. It is difficult to imagine a place more different from San Miguel de Allende than the Belgian capital. We are very attached to San Miguel de Allende, where we founded our company and where both our sons, Olivier and Antoine, were born and spent their early years. But as much as we loved our small town life in Mexico, Anne-Marie wanted the boys to have the experience of living in Europe, as she had done, and to be educated in French. After some deliberation, cosmopolitan Brussels—just an hour to Paris and two hours to London by Eurostar train—was our choice.

There were several things that appealed to us about Brussels. It is a diplomatic center where people speak many languages; we felt that our mixed-language family would blend in. The city has many parks and forests and wonderful architecture. In fact, the home of Victor Horta, the visionary Art Nouveau architect, is now a museum, located just a short walk from our townhouse. Belgium has always had an inspiring and active design scene, from the twentieth-century furniture designer Jules Wabbes (one of our favorites) to such contemporary taste-makers as the interior designer and antiques dealer Axel Vervoordt, the landscape designer

preceding spreads Venetian photograph albums, along with a collection of African Tutsi baskets found in Brussels, have been set on the surface of our "Branch" table in the middle of the living room. The fireplace—original to the house—is made of Arabescato marble (pages 26–27).

A detail of a 1950s painted tin tray from Mexico depicting parrots. The tray has been placed atop a stool to create a small side table. We were surprised to learn that a large parrot colony lives in our neighborhood. Every time we hear or see them in our garden, we are reminded of Mexico (pages 28–29).

opposite The nickel-framed "Opera" armchair, upholstered in a vintage Tehuantepec Mexican textile from the 1950s, has been placed in the white entry hall to add a punch of color. White paint was chosen to highlight the decorative plasterwork. The glass-paned doors, leading from the living to the dining areas, are original to the house and help to bring light into the middle of the townhouse floor.

above A partial view of the vestibule's double glass-paned front doors. They keep drafts from coming in and allow light to filter into the entry hall. My tokyobike is at the ready whenever the sun comes out. Hung on the wall above it is a watercolor of my grandmother at age sixteen. I chose an industrial light fixture that we found in Paris to contrast with the formal entryway.

Jacques Wirtz, and the housewares designer Michaël Verheyden.

In 2008, Anne-Marie went to Brussels in search of our new home. She was initially discouraged by what she found. Many of the available properties had been remodeled and this was reflected in their steep prices. Thanks to a tip from a childhood friend, she learned about an unlisted six-story townhouse on Avenue Molière, a grand boulevard of embassies and private residences. Built in 1907, the home had what Anne-Marie describes as "beautiful volumes of space" and, in the back, a long, rectangular walled garden. It was almost too large for our needs but she was smitten. The extra space would allow us each to maintain a home office, an ideal situation since we

opposite The living room's Roman window shades in a malachite cotton fabric by Tony Duquette for Jim Thompson are trimmed with grosgrain ribbon from Dedar. Chairs in a range of styles—from reproduction bergères to a cloister chair and an early twentieth-century Italian dining chair with a carved wood-and-caned back—surround the "Branch" coffee table. An iron *resplandor* (halo) from a traditional Mexican religious statue sits on the windowsill.

Above Placed on top of our "Andamio" table is a photograph by Sophie Ristelhueber, which leans against the wall. Printed on glass, it glows when backlit at night.

Opposite This multipurpose dining area is used not only for meals but also for doing homework and other activities. The bleached oak floor creates an informal ambience. Early twentieth-century Italian chairs and two "Ixelle Loop" settees have been placed around the glass-topped "Hiver" table. The crunched aluminum sculpture is by Peruvian artist Aldo Chaparro.

are parents of young children. Nevertheless, we'll never forget Anne-Marie's stepmother exclaiming on her first visit, "*Bonjour le chauffage!*" which roughly translates as "Wait until you get your heating bill!"

All things considered, the townhouse was in decent shape. We were very fortunate that many of the original details—the woodwork, decorative plasterwork, fireplace surrounds, and door handles—were all intact. The home's interior design was another story. The house had been decorated in a pastiche of French patterns, ranging from Empire to Provençal. The bathrooms and the kitchen were seriously due for remodeling. We also had falsely assumed that all the old-fashioned wallpapers could be easily removed. The challenges that lay ahead were daunting—not the least of which was creating an environment that would feel welcoming to a family accustomed to Mexico's endless sunshine.

Anne-Marie had grown up in Paris and was very familiar with the gloomy, dark winters that awaited us. She used her skills as a designer to devise ingenious ways to make our new home cheerful, bright, and intimate. She hired a local contractor in Brussels and directed the renovation long-distance from San Miguel. She chose a strong, saturated color palette to contrast with the bright white ceilings and millwork. Anne-Marie, who has a deep understanding of color theory, chose hues that would mesh perfectly with a room's function and exposure to light. For example, the northern rooms were painted in warm and earthy shades like oxblood and moss, while the southern-facing walls got a cooler palette of blue, white, and a pale lavender known in French as *parme*. The construction foreman

opposite I placed long curtains in a white Pierre Frey linen in the archway that separates the kitchen from the living area. I like the visual softness they create and the curtains can be drawn when I want to close off the kitchen from the adjoining living spaces. The gigantic broom-shaped hanging sculpture by San Miguel artist Susan Plum emphasizes the height of the ceiling. An amusing deer sculpture by Frédérique Morel, made of antique tapestry remnants, stands near the dining table.

above I turned the back parlor into a kitchen, which creates a more casual feeling within the formal setting of a historic townhouse. The wood cabinets have been painted in Flamant Dauphin in a satin finish. "Varenne" stools, upholstered in a Perennials outdoor fabric that allows for easy sponge cleanups, surround the kitchen island. The light fixture is a converted Parisian streetlamp, from Jérôme Lepert in Paris.

actually emailed Anne-Marie to ask whether the latter shade, destined for the library, was a mistake. The painters had told her that it looked ugly. "Please continue," Anne-Marie emailed back.

The layout of the townhouse was designed to work with our family's daily routine. With seven floors to climb, we did not want to spend time needlessly climbing and descending the stairs. The boys' playroom is located in the basement level within earshot of the kitchen one flight above. This is where they enter the house after school, play, do their homework, and then join us upstairs for dinner.

The townhouse's main living spaces are situated on the parlor floor. We converted the former dining room into a large and modern open kitchen with a bold yellow backsplash. (Nearby, the original galley kitchen was retained for extra storage and work areas.) The kitchen now adjoins a central parlor that functions as our dining room, which in turn connects to a pale gray living room. The windows have tailored Roman shades in a green malachite Tony Duquette cotton, which Anne-Marie had trimmed with black-and-gold borders. This floor is truly the heart of our home and has wonderful flexibility. We can grab breakfast at the kitchen's counters, enjoy intimate family dinners at the center table, or open the whole space up for larger parties.

The furnishings throughout the house are a mix of Casamidy creations, flea-market finds, inherited pieces, modern art, and pre-Columbian and Mexican artifacts. For instance, we decorated the living room with marquise-style armchairs from San Miguel, Italian wood chairs, a 1930s-style side table, a Casamidy sofa, and a gold-leafed iron halo that came from a traditional Mexican religious statue.

Up one flight, on the third floor, is our master bedroom, where a Casamidy "Diego" iron four-poster bed creates the illusion of a room within a room. We deliberately put our bedroom in the middle of the house for several reasons. The bedroom is connected to the library through a set of double doors. In the evening, we like to read or watch television in the library before heading to bed. What's more, we're just one flight down from the boys' shared bedroom and from Anne-Marie's home office. We can quickly attend to our responsibilities if we need to, and then, retreat back to our personal sanctuary.

On the fifth floor, our guest room hovers over the Brussels skyline. From the window, on a clear day you can see the Atomium, a building created for Expo 1958, the 1958 World's Fair, in the shape of an iron molecule, as well as the golden dome of the Palace of Justice. The bedroom's olive-brown shade complements the bed's green velvet headboard. This floor is also home to my studio, which has a skylight. I love to gaze upward at the passing sky with its shifting clouds and the occasional bursts of sun, which keeps me going through the long Brussels winters. We're high up at this point but there is even one more floor above us, an attic, which is not currently in use. Still, I can imagine the day in the future when our boys, entering their teen years, adopt it as their lofty lair.

The library has built-ins for storing books and displaying our many travel souvenirs, including hand-lacquered *maques* (hand-burnished gourds) from Pátzcuaro, Mexico. I customized an oversized tufted ottoman, which has been covered in cotton.

Initially I thought it would be a comfy place for our boys to relax; however, it is now covered with books and objects. My mother's armchairs have been reupholstered in French Catalan fabric from Les Toiles du Soleil.

With its southern exposure and almost perfect proportions, the library has been painted in *parme*, a pale violet. The double-length "Varenne" settee, covered in velvet, takes up one side of the room. I placed a "Hospicio" tin-framed mirror in silverleaf above the fireplace. Its dimensions have been exaggerated to play up the height of the ceiling. Flanking the fireplace are white alcoves displaying small paintings, drawings, and objects.

above The dressing area is adjacent to the master bedroom. Closing it off was not a viable option since the only source of natural light would be blocked. A wardrobe was built of black-tinted MDF composite. Its doors have been covered with Fornasetti wallpaper, which references the library next door. An outdoor light fixture is used indoors. I like the way it looks against the view of our backyard garden. I placed a glass-topped prototype of our round "Collier" table in the center of the room. The golden chains echo the gold details of the wallpaper (left). A friend gave me the idea of using an artist's easel to mount a television. I love this design solution and have used it in other places, too. The top of artist Mari Jose's worktable, which resembles a painting, hangs above the flat-screen TV (right).

opposite Our "Diego" canopy bed, inspired by the work of Diego Giacometti, one of our favorite furniture designers, has been personalized with the addition of a taut linen canopy, which is detailed with grosgrain ribbon of the same shade. The striped bed throw is from Zara Home. The boys enjoy sitting in my childhood home's antique iron-and-leather rocking chair.

opposite I covered our "Ixelle" wingback headboard in a pea-green velvet from J. B. Martin. The bed coverlet is from Turkmenistan; the side tables were found at Scènes de Ménage, an upscale vintage store in Brussels, near Place Brugmann. I always take the time to carefully consider where art should be hung. I think you need to live in a furnished room before nailing anything to the walls. Here, I framed the headboard by surrounding it with works of art. I also like to lean art against walls or set it on tables. The portrait of my grandmother, my own rubbings, and the ink drawing on the floor by Mic Killy create an interesting visual composition.

above The guest bedroom's color scheme is muted to evoke the earthy tones of the autumnal Belgian forest. The multicolored antique rug is from Turkey. The oak church-pew chair comes from La Belle Angerie, my grandmother's house in Normandy. The 1950s floor lamp is from La Savonnerie, a Brussels vintage furnishings store. The photograph is by Amber Eagle.

opposite I incorporated a comfortable reading spot in the boys' bedroom. A bed covered in an heirloom quilt serves as a sofa by day and provides extra sleeping space when the boys have a friend stay over. The large pillows are covered in Marimekko fabric and the smaller embroidered ones are from Oaxaca. An "Almidi" end table in bright yellow adds a touch of color, as does the boys' Lego collection.

above and left The bedroom walls are painted in a soothing Farrow & Ball Parma Gray. "Hospicio" headboards have been selected for the beds, which are covered in Ikea bed linens. I hung an old enameled sign for a Mexican oil product with an eye-catching rooster insignia between the beds. A French World War I biplane model bearing the French flag's colors hides the ceiling fixture. We found these metal British soldiers in London. We often take the boys to see the Waterloo battlefield, which is located in the countryside just eight miles south of Brussels. The historical importance of the site, where British and Prussian forces famously defeated Napoleon, is fascinating.

above On the landing of the boys' bedroom is a laundry basket made of car tires as well as a bench, purchased in Brussels, that was made with metal jerry cans. Above it is our friend Bill Killen's painting depicting the Mexican pyramids of Tajin, which was inspired by artist Walton Ford's work (left). In Brussels, our long and narrow backyard garden is known as a *jardin frite* because the elongated and skinny shape resembles a French fry. The leaves of the red beech-tree turn an incredible bright burgundy during the fall (right).

opposite We moved the playroom, which was originally located in the attic, to the basement so that it would have direct access to the garden. An extra-large laundry basket stores toys. Colorful child-size Mexican *equipales* chairs in painted pigskin leather are extremely durable. Since the boys share a bedroom, they each have their own bookcase here. I can imagine updating the room one day as a "teenager's" hangout, complete with an air hockey table and lounge chairs.

following spread A spare room on the top floor includes my grandmother's guest bed, constructed of Venetian wooden mooring posts. Next to it is our "Hiver" end table in nickel. An Ikea reading lamp is on top. A poster from my Rhode Island School of Design years hangs on the wall, and a painted portrait of my mother and me rests on the floor (left). To make the most of the smallest room in the house, I surrounded a queen-size bed with curtains in Yvan Puylaert's Designs of the Time fabric. This niche, used as a second guest room, is very cozy—in fact, it is a favorite of several of our friends. The console is from Afghanistan, and the little footrest is made of cane (right).

HOSPICIO
Our Design Laboratory

During our first three years in San Miguel de Allende, Anne-Marie and I lived in a funky house in the town's historic center. An open corridor framed by very high walls bordered the house. We created a pool in this space and tiled it in green glass mosaics. We planted cacti along the back wall in a kind of homage to the great Mexican modernist architect Luis Barragán. Unfortunately the pool became a dry-season watering hole for pigeons. The previous owner had covered the bedroom floors with glazed tile, which became very cold during the chilly evenings. After an especially frigid winter, we decided that it was time to find a new house.

We were focused on finding a Colonial-era *casita* (small house) but most of the available properties in town were dark and, to our eyes, overly ornate. Meanwhile, almost every day we walked by a somewhat forbidding-looking house perched on the hilly corner of Hospicio and Barranca Streets. It appeared to be a windowless box painted a generic peach color. The roof was encircled with chicken-wire fencing to prevent the owner's dogs from falling off the edge. A placard announced it was "*se vende*" (for sale). Curious, we called and scheduled a visit. When the door opened, Anne-Marie blurted out, "It smells like Lou Miedjou!" The scent reminded her of her beloved family house in the South of France.

preceding spread This long wooden church bench on the roof terrace of Hospicio, our home in San Miguel, is piled with pillows from Chiapas. Due to their constant exposure to the sun, they have bleached in an appealing way.

opposite The inside of the front door of Hospicio is covered with Mexican and Greek *milagros* and *retablos*. Over the door, a 1960s concrete niche is shaped like a scallop shell. I like the juxtaposition of the ex-votos with the overscale niche, which reminds me of the smaller niches displaying statuettes of saints that you often see in Mexican homes and churches. To the left of the door is a simple mail slot.

following spread Our living room continually changes. We treat it as our design laboratory, trying out our Casamidy prototypes here. Presently, we've placed our new "Loop" settee pieces in the room. I like to use two fabrics on a piece for variety—for the settee, red velvet on the front, and white linen on the back. The two armchairs are covered in the same linen on the front sides and a black-and-white striped fabric on the backsides. The oversized "Hacienda" coffee table is perfect for casual Mexican dinners. The fireplace, originally in pink cantera stone, was painted, which I felt harmonized better with the overall design scheme. The heavy window hardware is French, purchased from one of my favorite stores, the basement of the department store BHV.

We acquired it and now refer to it as Hospicio, after the name of the street on which it is located.

The house was built in the 1970s in a hybrid Franco-Mexican style that was very popular at the time in Mexico, particularly in Cuernavaca, where many people had weekend homes. We discovered that the home had several old adobe walls dating from the 1870s, when a previous building existed on the site. Inside, there was no shortage of windows. The home was flooded with sunlight and had sweeping views of town and the Sierra Morena mountains.

We furnished the house with antique French and Mexican furnishings, along with Casamidy pieces. In keeping with the spare Colonial architecture of San Miguel, we were very conscious of creating a feeling of restraint in the interiors of our house. To achieve this somewhat austere look, we stuck to a neutral palette and were careful not to overcrowd rooms with furniture. We placed ample space between pieces. It has required rigorous editing.

You can still find many beautiful religious objects in San Miguel. We find them irresistible —more for aesthetic than religious reasons— and have several objets. Anne-Marie transformed the home's nondescript large entry door by lining it in tin sheeting and ex-votos,

above, left and right Details from a previous living room decorating scheme. I like to mix different textures, such as old nickel and iron railway nails, and 1940s drip-glaze pottery with a pre-Columbian bowl.

opposite Italian chairs purchased in Mexico surround the "Hacienda" dining room table, which has a practical metal-clad surface. A 1950s Danish bronze light fixture hangs above. I never hesitate to mix different carved pieces together—the key is that they have related shapes or finishes. The nineteenth-century wooden altar pediment, stripped of its paint, adds depth to the room.

opposite The kitchen has a narrow backsplash in stoneware tiles from Ceramica Antique. The wall is decorated with Mexican ceramic plates from Pátzcuaro.

above This door leads to the garage and the kitchen. Next to it, a traditional painted Chinese cabinet was sanded to expose the wood underneath, giving it a whole new character that I felt was better suited for this house.

the colorful traditional offerings to saints and divinities that are popular in this devoutly Catholic part of Mexico. She was particularly inspired by the Parish of Immaculate Conception, a church in the nearby village of Real de Catorce. In that atmospheric building, the walls and doors are layered in folkloric depictions of miracles and gratitude for Saint Francis of Assisi.

Fortunately, Hospicio's terra-cotta floors had never been sealed or varnished and, as a result, had acquired an attractive patina from use. We maintain them by constant mopping and the occasional application of floor wax. For contrast with the dark floors, Anne-Marie

painted the interior walls in a stark white. What is unique about the paint treatment is that it is a standard latex paint mixed with lime wash, which creates a smooth, matte texture. The finish looks particularly striking when hit by sunlight, which streams through Hospicio's rooms during the day.

We created a large combination living-dining room on the home's main level. We love to gather with friends on the sofas and French-style chairs in front of the stone fireplace. The dining area is furnished with a Casamidy steel-topped "Hacienda" table, which was inspired by Mexican tin store counters. The antique dining chairs have seat cushions in a silk brocade, which contasts nicely with the contemporary

opposite I found a group of plaster Mexican architectural molds and turned them into wall art. I framed some of them in metal and added hooks to the ones with the more irregular shapes. I like the way the natural light strikes the patterned molds and creates varying shadows throughout the day.

above A collection of green pressed-glass vases in front of a Casamidy prism star-shaped mirror (left). A Pátzcuaro ceramic pineapple has an agave plant crown (middle). When we moved into the house, the scallop shell niches above the doorways were painted in a light shade of salmon. To make them less imposing, we matched them to the walls. Our small kitchen has terra-cotta tile floors and a large professional stove that we moved here when we closed our restaurant, Plum (right).

preceding spread In the gravel-lined courtyard, olive trees provide shade and buffer the street noise. The umbrellas are in Sunbrella outdoor fabric. I have another set in a contrasting color, a pinkish red. I swap them out when I want to change the mood and decor of the outdoor space.

opposite I converted a Mexican folk art—painted kitchen cupboard into a garden shed. It holds tools and containers for arranging bouquets and cleaning up the courtyard.

above For the outdoor dining area, I chose old country furniture instead of outdoor pieces—they relate to the interior furnishings. The wooden furniture is maintained by applying a matte UV protective lacquer once a year. I use large Santa Rosa candles, set on small dishes, to light up the courtyard at night. Smaller candles are placed in our "Symi" lanterns.

above The family room has built-in shelves, which we use to display our collection of Mexican folk art and other eclectic objects. There is a small gas fireplace below. The black 1950s chairs are from Jorge's family house in Culiacán (left). The small guest bathroom is tucked under the staircase. I purchased this locally carved *celosía* (lattice) of cantera stone that has an amusing decorative motif of a monkey. It is used here as a vent and to let in natural light (right).

opposite The master-suite terrace overlooks La Parroquia, San Miguel de Allende's Gothic-inspired church. We love to sit here and watch the town's many religious celebrations, which often include fireworks and colorful processions. The seating area is furnished with a mix of Casamidy pieces—"Varenne" chairs with a white powder coating, a "Symi" tray table, and Mexican *equipale* barrel chairs with hand-painted floral details. Potted plants ring the ledges of the balcony.

above The master bathroom doorway can be closed off with curtains made of jute, a natural material that can withstand splashes of water and sunlight (left). The room's focal point is a 1930s ceramic mural of Jorge's family's sugar refinery in Sinaloa, Mexico, which I had installed above the bathtub (right).

opposite For the master bedroom, I selected our "Hacienda" corrugated tin headboard. I like the way the silvery material reflects the light and almost glitters. Our "Andamio" bench is placed at the foot of the bed —it is a practical spot to pile books. The bed lights were suspended from the ceiling in order to free up space on the small bedside tables. The lamp's hanging chains were covered in jute fabric, for a softer look.

look of the table. Once again, we added some ecclesiastical touches purchased at a local antiques shop: a nineteenth-century carved church altar, stripped of its paint, and a large wooden statue of a saint.

From this space, one enters through a set of French doors into our version of a Mexican courtyard garden. Most Mexican gardens are situated on the ground level, but we created ours above the roof of the garage in order to maximize the sight lines. We lined the lush garden area with gravel and placed square stone floor tiles in the outdoor dining area. A wall fountain was installed and olive trees were planted to provide shade and privacy. We love to sit in the garden in the evening and enjoy the tranquility.

At the back of the courtyard is the family room, which doubles as Anne-Marie's work space. There is high shelving so that the children don't accidently break any of the fragile handmade objects and artwork that we treasure. Upstairs is our private quarters, which consist of a master bedroom and the boys' shared bedroom. A guest suite is located on the ground level next to the garden. These rooms are filled with handmade and personal touches. The master bedroom is furnished with an ornate tin headboard from our "Hacienda" line. In the bathroom, hanging over the bathtub is a tiled 1920s mural depicting my family's former sugar refinery. The boys' bedroom has a pair of narrow four-poster beds and a Gothic-style bookcase.

The top of the *casita* has a great view of town, and so we couldn't resist adding a rooftop terrace. There, an arbor shelters the outdoor chaise seating, while our Casamidy lanterns line the edges of the space. We love to relax here while gazing out at the Gothic spire of La Parroquia church, or looking down at San Miguel's cobblestone streets lined with buildings painted in sunny shades like ocher, rust, and yellow.

Hospicio is a very meaningful home for Anne-Marie and me. It is where we started our interior and furniture design business. The house is our design laboratory. To this day, we test all of our new Casamidy furnishings here. It is also where we became parents. Our sons, Olivier and Antoine, were born here in 2005 and 2006, in the space of just fifteen months. Hospicio was their home for the first years of their lives. We still spend summers and holidays here, even now that we live in Brussels. Like its name, which means "hospice" in Spanish, this warm and joyful home provides our little family with a sense of solace. It remains a deeply personal refuge both for us and for our boys.

The minute I spotted this whimsical Gothic-style bookcase at a local antiques store, Casa Reyna, I knew I had to have it. I applied a light bluish-gray wash over the original very dark brown color. The piece now lives in the boys' bedroom.

In the boys' bedroom, the floor is covered in classic green-and-white Mexican tile with a *paloma* (dove) motif combined with unglazed terra-cotta rectangles. Most of the furniture was found in antiques shops and converted to fit the boys' needs. Between the beds, the night table—which I think came out of a hardware store—today doubles as a bin for stuffed animals. Above it is Kent Rogowski's photograph of an inside-out teddy bear. An antique shelving unit from a hardware store now functions as a storage area for toys. A table was created from a simple wooden base topped with a recycled table surface. Jorge designed the leather rocking horse for Olivier's first birthday. The beds have green canopies, which coordinate with the color of the floor tile and the nearby bathroom. On the beds, hand-embroidered pillows are decorated with images from the popular Mexican children's game *lotería*.

above The doors in the guest bedroom have a dark-blue wash enhanced by a layer of wax, which creates a sense of depth. A second doorway was closed off and fitted with built-in drawers and shelving. At the foot of the bed is a wooden trunk with a star-patterned tin decoration. The linen slipcovered headboard is framed by a pair of sconces that I purchased at La Lagunilla, the flea market in Mexico City. The ceiling beams have been whitewashed and waxed.

above and opposite My goal with the guest bathroom, which faces the garden, was to create a space that feels unexpected. I found a wonderful vintage cast-iron tub, complete with the original faucet and soap dish, and installed it in front of the window. The paneled screen, made of iron and string, separates the bath from the dressing area. While the room is equipped with an electric light, it also has antique wall sconces that hold candles. A church column has been converted into a cabinet for stashing hand towels and extra soaps.

The roof terrace is most often used during the winter months, when the weather can be cool and a dose of direct sunlight can be warming. In the evening, we enjoy the expansive views of San Miguel and the surrounding countryside from the terrace, which is furnished with our "Maroma" lounge chairs as well as olive bushes and lavender in clay pots. Agave plants serve as a natural wind and safety barrier along the rooftop's edge. A variety of rustic Mexican stools function as side tables (my favorite is the one shaped like a cat). To shelter the terrace from the bright sunshine, taut strips of henequen in natural and pink were attached with Velcro onto an iron armature. At nighttime, we light the "Symi" lanterns that have been lined up in a row. An oversized lantern helps to illuminate the seating area.

SOLLANO
A Twist on Tradition

We moved to San Miguel de Allende to expand our design business, Casamidy. But shortly after arriving in town, we decided to join forces with a couple from Corsica to open a bistro. We hoped that the restaurant, which we called Plum, would be a comfortable gathering place for both locals and foreigners while also serving as a showcase for our furniture and design aesthetic.

We were to oversee the visual aspects of the restaurant, with our partners managing the kitchen and the bar. In keeping with the bistro's name, we painted the space in various shades of purple. We designed tables and chairs in polished aluminum and created banquettes whose shape was inspired by the benches in vintage Parisian subway cars. Unfortunately, the other couple thought our design scheme was hideous and quickly opted out of the venture. We found ourselves with a restaurant and not much of a clue of how to run it.

After a failed attempt to hire a chef, Anne-Marie called her friend Joseline Snajder, a talented cook who had been employed by her family for many years at their country home in Saint-Paul-de-Vence in France. She was kind enough to share a few simple recipes, including her wonderful *tarte à l'oignon* and a tapenade in which whiskey is the secret ingredient. Anne-Marie headed to the bistro's kitchen to prepare those dishes for our

In a traditional Mexican hacienda, furniture would have been kept to a minimum. I used the same approach at Casa Sollano, where I also took the opportunity to showcase Mexican artisanal pieces. A stone wall, original to the house, is the dominant element in this home office. The simplicity of the furnishings—a Mexican pine cabinet that serves as a console, a lamp base that was fashioned from a large glass bottle—contrasts with the boldness of the architectural backdrop. For visual interest, I mounted an instructional 1930s calendar illustrating the founding figures of the state of Guanajuato on a board and had it framed. A salvaged old drawer holds the house's floor plans.

opposite An elegant stone fireplace provides a focal point in the living room, which has a classic furniture layout. Agapanthus flowers—single stems placed in small glass containers—are lined up on the mantelpiece. I like the way they reflect the rhythm of the fireplace's carvings and soften the room's austere atmosphere. A Moroccan rug—straw with wool embroidery—has the same effect. I always think smaller pieces look wonderful in a large room—the contrast helps to accentuate the oversized scale of the space. Here, I deliberately included some diminutive pieces, including Jorge's reproduction of his grandmother's small black armchairs, as well as the tiny rustic stool next to the sofa. These were combined with such bolder statements as a huge and elongated vintage sugar mold, which I placed on the wall as sculpture. Natural fabrics—henequen, linen, and cotton—are used throughout the house.

above The carved wood doors and ceiling beams (seen on page 83)—both original to the house—were whitewashed to brighten the interior spaces. In the living room, the Colonial-era armoire, which retains its original paint, has simple lines that complement the carved grid shapes on the entry doors.

Henequen strips are stretched across the patio to filter the bright outdoor daylight. I incorporated a fountain into one of the archways. The water flows into a trough, a functional element found in many traditional haciendas. The ledge is wide enough to accommodate candles, which are used to light up the fountain at night. To help the new stone structure to blend into the home's older architecture, I planted a climbing vine, which does not grow too thickly or flower, at the base of the fountain wall. The day this photograph was taken, a pair of donkeys arrived to make their weekly firewood delivery to the house—a San Miguel tradition.

customers, along with mini hamburgers that she served on Mexican *bolillo* bread and cocktails inspired by Harry's Bar in Venice. Meanwhile, I oversaw the front of the house and the bar.

At its height, Plum was a lot of fun. Everyone came through our doors, from San Miguel locals to artists from Mexico City to American expats. But as much they seemed to enjoy both the food and the decor, few people seemed to think that our design aesthetic would translate to their own homes. That is, until one day a Bostonian named Dorsey R. Gardner arrived at the restaurant to offer Anne-Marie her first major interior design project—the renovation of a large 1780s villa on Sollano Street. With a background in finance, Gardner was also an artist who wanted to set up his painting studio in San Miguel.

Casa Sollano is one of the last grand and largely intact houses in town. Certainly, it is one of the few that has expansive views from the ground floor. The home's front door opens through an archway onto a magnificent vista of the nearby valley. What's more, the house is bathed in sunlight throughout much of the day. It was designed around a layout that is typical in this temperate part of Mexico, with rooms accessed through exterior colonnades surrounding a vast patio. You have to step outside in order to walk from room to room. The property also came with an orchid house. Gardner's design team included Anne-Marie and a top-notch local builder, Sebastián Zavala. They streamlined the main house into a three-bedroom artist's retreat. Zavala added a small, stone-walled studio for Gardner in the lower courtyard. He also reconfigured an existing building in the lower garden into a loggia for entertaining. In addition, a large sunken

above The kitchen wall has blue-and-white Talavera tile in a zigzag pattern that adds a contemporary element to the traditional house. We bought the tile in the nearby town of Dolores Hidalgo. The wood cabinets were whitewashed. I spent a long time choosing the color of this room, which is red. For me, getting the color right is essential. I paint swatches directly on the wall, as I did in this case, or on large sheets of paper that I hang on the wall. This enables me to see how colors are affected by direct and artificial light, as well as how they look in shade.

opposite The dining room is framed by French doors and can appear quite dramatic when light streams in throughout the day. I hung an overscale oval "Hacienda" mirror to give the illusion that the space is larger than it actually is.

above For the master bathroom, which has a very high ceiling, I designed an oversized mirror inspired by antique Venetian mirrors. A medicine cabinet is hidden behind one of the mirrored panels. A thick slab of cantera stone has been used for the countertop and the double sinks (left). The dressing room is tucked between the bathroom and the bedroom, creating a transition between these two areas (right).

opposite The master bedroom still retains its original stucco walls. The blue linen bedspread picks up the color of the room's antique wall frieze.

garden, a rarity in this part of town where land is at a premium, was created at the suggestion of Anne-Marie.

Having traveled extensively in Mexico, Anne-Marie had seen quite a lot of Spanish Colonial architecture. In that period, houses were constructed of stone and adobe brick with wooden details. The wall surfaces were then covered with plaster, which breathes and therefore enables water to evaporate after the rainy season, preserving the wooden and brick elements from damage. The rooms in these

homes were supposed to be sparse; they were never intended to be crowded with furniture or covered up in wallpaper. But as fashions changed, the interiors of these homes had evolved and become far more decorative than was the original intent. To us, one of the saddest things is when we see a Colonial home where the plaster has been sealed behind layers of cement and shiny latex paint (and usually paired with dark curtains and heavy, ornate furniture.)

Anne-Marie went in the opposite direction and specified that the walls be coated in artisanal plaster and lime wash. During the renovation, the restorers opened up the walls and discovered the original fresco decorative wall banding. This was restored and now melds beautifully with the new plaster walls, as would have been the case when the house was first constructed.

Anne-Marie decorated the house with a combination of antiques and new furnishings. She transformed antique zinc store counters into headboards—at twelve feet in length, their size pairs well with the large rooms. She furnished the house primarily with local materials, including jute, linen, henequen, and saddle leather. To create an overall atmosphere of air and light, she used a light palette of pale neutrals. The massive ceiling beams were white-washed and the carved wooden doors were bleached. Diaphanous henequen draperies were stretched across the patio in order to diffuse the sunlight,

which can be strong at midday. To balance the tall height of the ceiling in the living room, she designed oversized ceiling fixtures and furniture that was deliberately low-slung. She also mixed materials throughout the home. In the dining room, for instance, she put a modern stainless-steel top on a rustic table. The kitchen has a Talavera tile backdrop that is set off by hand-hewn wood cabinetry.

The Colonial-style patio is a sheltered space located in the heart of the house, which serves to regulate light and heat. In San Miguel this feature remains constant, whether a home is grand or humble. Casa Sollano may possibly have the best patio in the city—surrounded by double-height walls, the open-air space has a large arch that opens onto a lovely vista of San Miguel and La Sierra Morena mountain range. The house also has courtyards that have been landscaped with border grasses, bougainvillea, lavender, and pepper as well as fruit-bearing trees.

We ended up closing Plum after a couple of years for a variety of reasons, including a falling-out with a landlord. But we have no regrets. While the idea of showcasing our design work in a restaurant setting was a bit of a bust, the one client who did respond to it handed Anne-Marie her first professional interior design project, which is still one of our favorites. Casa Sollano was widely published and helped Casamidy to grow into the design firm it is today.

opposite This covered patio overlooks the garden. As the sun can be blinding, I created sliding henequen curtain panels that can be closed for shade and privacy. The chairs are made of woven leather that requires periodic oiling. The wine cooler and roll-up backgammon set are from the first Casamidy accessories collection.

following spread The stone patio, replete with an oversized iris bush and an orange tree, was installed during the renovation (left). The upstairs guest bedroom opens onto a terrace. The entry can be closed off with curtains. Rather than curtains, I covered the windows with linen panels attached with Velcro to metal frames. A *batea* (wooden container for grain storage) set on an old trunk at the foot of the bed is used to store magazines and newspapers. Part of a traditional Oaxacan chair is in view (right).

The art studio has wonderful light and is furnished simply with pieces such as a metal-framed daybed. The easel has been placed on a *petate*, a traditional Mexican floor matting that is woven in straw.

95

CASA PALIKAO
A Mexican Colonial Home

Casa Palikao is an eighteenth-century house, full of grand archways and dramatic colonnades, that occupies a coveted location in the center of San Miguel de Allende. The home was purchased by a couple from France. They were drawn to San Miguel's enchanting hilltop setting, historic architecture, and the close-knit international community. They chose a house that is located in a neighborhood bustling with activity because it reminded them of Oran, the wife's original North African hometown in Algeria. In this commercial part of town, with its shoe shops and pharmacies, one would never know that their spacious house is nestled behind a façade of thick plaster walls.

When the wife first saw it, the sheltered design of this historic home seemed reminiscent of the Algerian architecture she remembered from her youth. She named this house Casa Palikao after a property owned by her family when she was a child. The building was in good structural condition and Anne-Marie was hired to help with a light renovation and to refresh the interior design.

Outside of Mexico, people sometimes refer to a grand home such as this one as a hacienda, but that's a misnomer. The countryside near San Miguel has many haciendas, which are larger ranch-like properties devoted to producing everything from pulque, an alcoholic beverage,

The embossed leather daybed was made in Querétaro by artisans skilled in bookbinding. The design is based on a vintage piece that I bought at auction. The cotton muslin throw—which is known as a *tenango*—was hand-embroidered by Otomi Indians in the Mexican state of Hidalgo. Displayed on the mantel are ceramic figures from Michoacán and a tin *árbol de la vida* (tree of life).

The exterior living room is furnished with traditional hacienda furniture and two clay outdoor fireplaces, which are lit on chilly nights. A wood plank bench is set inside an archway. A grouping of tin star lights, which are made locally, hangs from the beamed ceiling. They cast patterned shadows on the walls at night.

The owners, who often entertain, made the bold decision to replace the patio with a large pool. It was crafted in polished cement and framed by cantera stone edges that are wide enough to sit on. The pool is surrounded by palm trees and feels like an oasis in the heart of the house.

red (the hue was inspired by the interior of a watermelon). This was balanced with the quieter tones she chose for the wall color in the larger rooms, as well as for the fabrics and furniture throughout.

Anne-Marie furnished the home with understated pieces, including rustic furnishings purchased from local antiques vendors on San Miguel's Hidalgo Street. Curtains in natural cotton were hung from arches in the long hallways to create a feeling of intimacy as well as a marked transition from space to space. The living room floor had large, irregular-shaped stones that tended to get chilly during the winter. To remedy the situation, we designed a large rug out of squares of raw saddle leather backed in rubber and joined together with leather ties. The edge of the rug has a whipstitch-braided detail traditionally used on Mexican saddles. Traditional Mexican *artesanía*, including ceramics from the village of Tzintzuntzan, Michoacán, were placed throughout the home as decorative accents.

The homeowners hold an annual Bastille Day party at Casa Palikao for family and friends. On that day, people of all ages and nationalities gather in the courtyard, which is lit with tin star-shaped lights, and dine at long tables placed in the corridors of the house. Anne-Marie and I always look forward to this festive evening, when San Miguel locals and the expatriate community come together with openness in an unforgettable setting.

above An array of gourds, ropes, and market bags greets visitors in the entranceway to the home.

opposite Tin star lights hang in the courtyard's soaring arched colonnade. The entrance to the bedroom is marked with two Colonial tables that are topped with wooden *bateas* filled with fresh-cut flowers.

For the upstairs bedroom, I designed fabric headboards and edged the sides with oversized nails designed as door hardware. I tried to amplify the calm, monastic feel of the room by keeping the palette simple—even the embroidery on the artisanal bedcovers is in a neutral tone.

PARIS

RUE DE CONDÉ
A Left Bank Pied-à-Terre

preceding spread This photograph of a view of Parisian rooftops was taken from the balcony of our apartment in the Marais's Hôtel d'Hallwyl. Though I lived in another arrondissement when I was a teenager, it reminds me of late nights studying for my baccalaureate.

opposite The shelving on the left originally had doors, which I removed. I use it to display personal objects, including several that I inherited from my late mother. The mahogany library ladder is by David Hicks. A smart design, it folds into a vertical rod that can be leaned against the wall.

When Anne-Marie turned eighteen, her grandmother Monique Manchez Midy gifted her a tiny apartment on Rue de Condé on the Left Bank of Paris. The building, a 1612 *hôtel particulier* (townhouse) that had been converted into apartments in the 1920s, has been home to various members of her extended family for many years. There are four main apartments in the building, two of which belong to Anne-Marie's aunts and a third to her brother Emmanuel.

This serene Parisian flat is in a wonderful location halfway between Saint-Germain-des-Prés and the Luxembourg Gardens. To get to the third-floor apartment, one enters a tiny oak-paneled elevator, which is enclosed in a wrought-iron cage next to the stairwell. As a teenager, Anne-Marie was thrilled with her grandmother's generous gift. The apartment was filled with light and had a decorative plaster ceiling dating from the nineteenth century. At the time she was given it, the walls were Barbie doll–pink with a brown ribbon detail. The carpeting was pink, too. She toned it down with basic white canvas window treatments and slipcovers and kept it that way for more than a decade.

At five hundred square feet, it was the perfect compact home for a young woman in her early twenties. The layout consisted of two

small rooms—a living room and a bedroom—separated by a dividing wall. A small galley kitchen was located through glass-paneled doors in the entry hall.

After I entered the picture, we would make regular visits to Paris. The apartment was just big enough for the two of us. At this point, Anne-Marie devised a second color scheme. This time she painted the apartment in varying shades of blue offset by a coral entry hall. When her mother passed away in 1999, Anne-Marie inherited her paintings, prints, antiques, and flea-market treasures and incorporated them into the decor. Fortunately, the apartment's height afforded lots of wall space for hanging her mother's art collection.

But the years passed and with the arrival of our two boys, Rue de Condé's tight squeeze was no longer viable for a family of four. We found a larger apartment in the Marais. But since we often rent out the new apartment out, we still needed a Parisian pied-à-terre for when one of us is in town. To make it more comfortable, a few years ago we decided to remove the dividing wall. During the demolition, we opened the ceiling and were ecstatic to discover that the original roughhewn oak roof beams were intact. We loved them and decided to leave them exposed, which is as they would have been.

With the wall removed, the space felt exponentially bigger. We placed a custom-made bed in the center of the room and anchored it with a minimalist headboard in order to delineate between the sleeping and seating areas. We installed a modern galley kitchen and enlarged the bathroom, transforming it with white marble into a much brighter space. The color palette was kept simple—mostly whites

above In the living room, the Austrian opera chairs, which date from the early nineteenth century, are upholstered in a canary-yellow fabric. The room's furnishings include a vintage leather-and-iron cocktail table and an iron floor lamp, a Paris flea-market find.

opposite A view from the apartment's entrance. Even though the hallway is quite narrow, I was able to fit a chair in the space. I use it as a handy surface for mail and keys. The painting that hangs above the doorway is by my friend Karen Cho.

An apartment this small has to be well edited. The armless Muji sofa can be pressed into service as a guest bed. While the floor space is limited, the tall walls presented an opportunity to hang quite a bit of art. I centered a large piece above the sofa and surrounded it with smaller works. I even succeeded in hanging two favorite paintings—an abstract fish by Anne Pesce and a portrait of a mother and child by Sylvie Gronnier—on top of the mantel mirror. I like how they interact with the reflection. I also had to get creative about storage. I hide a file organizer in the nonworking fireplace. No one would know because it is hidden behind an upholstered jute screen, which I dressed up by stenciling it with a floral pattern.

and grays, with accents of red and blue—so that the massive ceiling beams would stand out.

In this chapter, we have decided to show images of the Rue de Condé apartment before and after the most recent renovation. In truth, though we still sometimes reminisce about how intimate the apartment used to feel, the new, more contemporary direction and open floor plan has resulted in a more functional and enjoyable space to inhabit. Our Rue de Condé apartment is far more comfortable now and the simplicity of the design feels somehow more in tune with the high-ceilinged grandeur of the original seventeenth-century architecture.

left My grandmother's Italian Baroque bed with its blue-frescoed headboard is a statement piece. The vibrant hue inspired the room's color scheme, which is multiple shades of blue. In keeping with the theme, I displayed a collection of blue-and-white Chinese dishes on a wall. I like to cover part of the bed with a textured quilt to break up the whiteness of the sheets. Above the radiator hangs an etching of a Madonna by my grandmother, which was given to me at birth, and her vintage Lanvin perfume bottles have been placed on a shelf in the corner.

opposite The apartment's furnishings include several inherited pieces and one of our Casamidy "Opera" side chairs. On top of the dresser are vintage metal molds in the shapes of a fork and a spoon, which I found at the Paris flea market.

THE
RENOVATION

opposite I decorated the mantel with a postcard
of Venice and family photographs from the 1940s.

above, clockwise from top left Michal Marucha,
our contractor, and I wait at the front entrance
of the building during the apartment's renovation.
We discovered these seventeenth-century beams
during the demolition. The original front door to the
apartment, with this classic doorknob, was left intact.

opposite Since the apartment lacks closet space, I needed a storage solution and came up with this custom-made armoire. I draped a large scarf over the opening, which takes up less space than a door. The bed's headboard is covered in a Fornasetti wallpaper, Nuvolette, resembling clouds. The headboard was designed to create a divider between the room's public and private areas. The living area in front of the bed is furnished with a pair of French hand-carved wooden chairs with a chinoiserie-style appliqué.

above I installed a galley kitchen with Silestone countertops in the entry passageway. In Europe you can find compact appliances for small quarters. I was able to fit a washer/dryer, a refrigerator, a microwave/oven, a sink, two induction burners, and upper cabinets into this space. I also squeezed cabinets under the windows for storing glasses and nicknacks. The cabinets have soft leather-loop pulls so that if anyone bumps into them, he or she won't get bruised.

124

above A Casamidy "Bistro" table sits in front of
a metal-framed couch in the apartment's living area.
Chilean artist Cristobal Gajardo's Bic-pen reproduction
of a Goya painting hangs above the couch (left).
This graceful iron detail, dating from the nineteenth
century, adorns the window railing (right).

opposite The shelves have been edged with marbleized
paper customarily used for bookbinding. I like the way this
discreet touch adds a soft textural element to the design.
The objects on display include a kitchen pitcher, a vase from
the Dutch company Wonderable, a Mariages Frères tea
container, assorted trays, books, and decorative objects.

HÔTEL D'HALLWYL
A Rooftop Oasis

If you were to ask Anne-Marie today where she is from, she would likely say, "I'm from Paris but I'm a Mexican at heart." Still, she can't stay away from her native Paris for long. Since Paris is so near to Brussels, she is able to circle back often to visit her Parisian family and friends. She also derives much inspiration from the beauty and creativity of her hometown.

Anne-Marie's first Paris apartment was on the Left Bank. When we started looking for a larger one to accommodate our family of four, we decided to search on the Right Bank. Our fantasy was to find an apartment in a pre-Revolutionary *hôtel particulier*. Indeed, we found just such a space: a unique apartment in the Haut-Marais, a historic district in Paris's 3rd arrondissement. The building, called the Hôtel d'Hallwyl, is the former residence of Jacques Necker, the Swiss-born finance minister of Louis XVI. This magnificent edifice is the only surviving example of domestic architecture in Paris by the noted French Neoclassical architect Claude-Nicolas Ledoux. He was commissioned to build it in 1766 by Franz-Joseph d'Hallwyl, a colonel of the Swiss Guard.

For us, it was love at first sight when we saw the front entrance, with its carved-wood doors and a stone tympanum carved with images of Greek goddesses. Inside, an interior courtyard is paved with stones leading to a swooping grand

The Hôtel d'Hallwyl's magnificent façade is adorned with a stone tympanum sculpted with images of goddesses. Infused with history, the building was the birthplace of Madame de Staël, a prominent French woman of letters who lived here with her father Jacques Necker, who was the minister of finance to Louis XVI. During the French Revolution, they abandoned their home. Whenever I enter the grand staircase, I can't help but imagine how they lived here before those troubled times that changed the course of French history.

following spread The apartment is located under the building's roofline. The structural beams have been whitewashed. If you look closely, you can see the faint marks of initials carved into the beams. I often wonder if they date back to when the building was erected, between 1766 and 1770. Since the dining and living areas share a common space, I decided to use the benches as seating around the dining table rather than chairs to avoid having too many "legs" in the room. The "Altamura" sofa brings versatility to the room because it doubles as an extra single bed.

above and opposite After crossing the interior courtyard, one arrives at the building's grand staircase. Its ironwork, dating from the eighteenth century, survived the Revolution. The wall is painted in a trompe-l'oeil that resembles stone. Even though the building has an elevator, which is concealed behind a small door, I prefer to use the stairs. The scale of each step is perfection, which makes for an easy climb to our apartment.

staircase and hallways with elegant sandstone walls. Our apartment, which is located on the fourth floor under the roof's dormers, has a striking angularity. Our little terrace has views of the Marais's zinc-clad rooftops. On the other side, we can glimpse the nearby Centre Pompidou through our windows. Our boys call the apartment "Le Bateau" because the shape of the space resembles the inverted hull of a ship. The ceiling is held up by a lattice of

massive oak beams. The walls bend at odd angles, reflecting the peaked shape of the roof above.

The building had gone through a gut renovation in the early 1990s, which meant that we did not have to take on the large task of a structural remodeling. Unfortunately, the architecture had assumed a generic feeling because of the addition of drywall. We felt the easiest way to add depth and character to the interior was with paint. Because the apartment

above To soften the hallway entrance, I hung curtains in gray linen that has been backed in silk taffeta. The tieback is made of old chains and metal pom-pons. The table faces the kitchen's pass-through. I have considered opening it up but valuable counter and storage space would be lost. The paintings depicting a pineapple and a cucumber were among the first art purchases I made, when I was in my teens. Fornasetti plates are displayed on the console.

opposite The cozy terrace has a classic zinc railing and a balustrade on three sides. We often enjoy morning coffees, dinner, or drinks here. The aluminum chairs are light and require little maintenance. The view of the French rooftops is always memorable—on a sunny or cloudy day, I can stare out at the city for hours.

opposite A charcoal drawing by my grandmother with a quote describing what it feels like to be in a badmood. A photograph taken of my great-grandfather during World War I leans against it.

above, clockwise from top left A reproduction of the 1785 Dominique Doncre painting *Petit Chien Jouant Avec un Soulier*, from Paris's Musée de la Chasse et de la Nature. Its palette inspired the color scheme of the apartment. I placed this small piece of furniture inside the entrance for leaving keys or messages. My grandmother sculpted the torso inside the Mexican mid-century ceramic bowl. A tool board hangs on the wall. A tableau on a shelf contains an assortment of eggs—ostrich, marble, tin, and painted wooden ones—with my childhood copy of *Fables de la Fontaine* as the backdrop. The bedroom shades are made from felt (originally all black) purchased at the BHV department store. I cut the felt to size and sewed it with thick yarn. After a season in the sunlight, the felt faded and now looks as though it was deliberately printed in this way.

136

has many windows and skylights, the color is always shifting depending on the season or the time of day. We are big fans of the highly pigmented paints of the British firm Farrow & Ball, since many of their hues have natural mineral pigments.

The palette we came up with was inspired by the painting *Petit Chien Jouant Avec un Soulier* by Dominique Doncre, dated 1785, that we saw at the Musée de la Chasse et de la Nature, a very original museum in the Marais. We painted most of the apartment in Farrow & Ball's All White, while select feature walls were covered in London Clay, a richly saturated shade with variant aspects of purple, gray, and brown. The third color, a dusty pink called Cinder Rose, was used as an accent hue inside the living room's bookshelves, where Anne-Marie displays books and objects.

opposite From this window, one has a glimpse of the Centre Pompidou. An Italian glass barometer is displayed on the windowsill. I remember watching the glass bubbles go up or down depending on the weather when I was a child, and now my boys are equally fascinated.

above One of our boys' fish drawings is displayed on a "Condé" desk, which is paired with a "Montelargo" chair. I like the way the large nickel grommets complement the iron desk. A flea-market milk crate holds postcards and dried flowers. To the left of the desk, a structural beam is used to display favorite postcards. A recycled metal kitchen pot holds odds and ends (left).

The apartment's layout consists of a large common area, a small kitchen, and two bedrooms. Because we have kids and rent out the apartment when we are not there, we wanted the design of the space to be flexible and informal, along the lines of a beach house. The common room was divided into zones for living and dining. The living area was furnished with our "Altamura" sectional sofa, upholstered in soft Mexican waxed cotton, a durable fabric that is easy to clean. The large sisal rugs covering the floors are also hard wearing and water-repellent. From Muskhane, a nearby shop, Anne-Marie purchased felt cashmere rugs in hot pink and ocher, placing them throughout the apartment to add punches of color. In the dining area, a copper-topped Casamidy wooden table is paired with walnut benches found at the Marché aux Puces in Paris.

In Europe, you often see kitchens and bathrooms that have been modernized and so seem out of place within historic interiors. That was the case here: the apartment's kitchen and bathrooms were very basic. We did not want to break the bank and decided to update the bathrooms first. Anne-Marie had the master bathroom retiled in an octagonal stone, which creates a visual link with the antique octagonal terra-cotta tile used on the building's landings. We would love to renovate the kitchen and have thought about removing the wall that separates it from the common area.

Our master bedroom, located in the rear of the apartment, feels very private. Anne-Marie furnished it with an exceptional piece: an eighteenth-century cobalt and silver-leaf headboard that her grandmother purchased in Venice. Although it's Italian, we like that it

above To the side of the framed drawing by Paul César Helleu are decorative Mexican wax-flower candles. Don't they look as if they belong on her hat?

opposite Much of the furniture in this room, including the antique bed, was moved here from our Rue de Condé apartment. Sometimes furniture retains its personality, but in a different space it can assume a fresh attitude, as I think it does here. A small reading lamp is clamped to the edge of the marble bedside table, a solution that I like because it doesn't take up too much space. A vintage Louis Vuitton suitcase is used for storing items such as blankets.

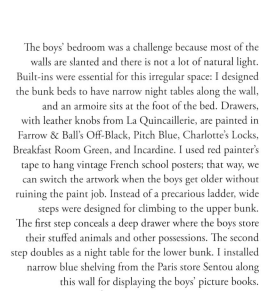

The boys' bedroom was a challenge because most of the walls are slanted and there is not a lot of natural light. Built-ins were essential for this irregular space: I designed the bunk beds to have narrow night tables along the wall, and an armoire sits at the foot of the bed. Drawers, with leather knobs from La Quincaillerie, are painted in Farrow & Ball's Off-Black, Pitch Blue, Charlotte's Locks, Breakfast Room Green, and Incardine. I used red painter's tape to hang vintage French school posters; that way, we can switch the artwork when the boys get older without ruining the paint job. Instead of a precarious ladder, wide steps were designed for climbing to the upper bunk. The first step conceals a deep drawer where the boys store their stuffed animals and other possessions. The second step doubles as a night table for the lower bunk. I installed narrow blue shelving from the Paris store Sentou along this wall for displaying the boys' picture books.

dates to the same period as the building, even if its Baroque styling is very different from Ledoux's Neoclassical architectural motifs.

The biggest challenge was the boys' room, which is extremely narrow, and has a slanted wall and two doors, and no closet. We also did not want to obstruct the natural light. Anne-Marie came up with a clever solution. On the sloped wall she created a built-in dresser, thereby making an unusable space functional. She also designed a bunk bed with an integrated armoire for hanging clothes and coats.

Our Marais apartment has proven to be a wonderful place for our family to stay during our regular visits to Paris. We enjoy the Haut-Marais, which is filled with specialty food shops, art galleries, and small restaurants, as well as museums like the Carnavalet and the Musée Picasso. From here, with the boys on their scooters, we can easily traverse the Seine and explore central Paris without ever really needing to take the Métro or a taxi. Each time that we return to the Hôtel d'Hallwyl and open its massive carriage doors to enter the paved court and the ground-floor garden just behind it, we're astonished that such a place exists in the very center of an urban metropolis.

above A large walk-in shower has been installed in the master bath. The wall is covered in large stone tile, while the floor features a combination of Kesra brown limestone and cement hexagon tile. The Vero sink from Duravit has a simple profile that suits the space.

opposite The entrance to the boys' bathroom used to have a door. The armoire in their room now functions as a divider. The walls are tiled in Tenthirty Faience tile from Carrelages des Suds, which has a gleaming finish that reflects the natural light. The floor is tiled in a mix of polished and un-polished hexagon toile (or *tomettes*, as they are called in France). Duravit's Happy D sink has rounded corners that make it kid friendly.

SAINT-PAUL-DE-VENCE

LOU MIEDJOU
An Intimate Family Villa

preceding spread Two bouquets
of lavender cut from the garden have
been set on an old tapestry chair.
They remind everyone not to sit on
this fragile piece of furniture.

opposite Original to the house,
Provençal tile is used as a background
for this water faucet on the loggia.
Today this spot is used as a jardinière.

following spread A view of the
medieval town of Saint-Paul-de-
Vence. The home's carved-wooden
front door has a distinctive detail:
an oversized lock and key. The latter
casts a shadow shaped like a heart
in the early afternoon (right).

In the 1920s, Anne-Marie's great-grandfather
Marcel Midy built a villa in the artist's village
of Saint-Paul-de-Vence on the French Riviera.
He was a Parisian born to a family whose
pharmaceutical business, Laboratoires Midy,
has a history going back to eighteenth-century
France. He always loved art and collected it.
After World War I, in which he had served as
a member of the French medical corps, Marcel
purchased a plot of land in Saint-Paul-de-Vence
from the Roux family, owners of La Colombe
d'Or, the beautiful restaurant and inn where
the interiors and gardens are graced with works
of art by Matisse, Picasso, Calder, Léger, Cézanne,
and other notable artists. He called the villa
Lou Miedjou, which means "noon" in the old
Provençal dialect. It's also a playful reference
to the family's surname since "*midi*" means
"noon" in French.

The villa was purposely built on a small scale.
Perhaps Anne-Marie's great-grandfather—one of
the first Parisians to build a home in the area—
did not want to draw too much attention to his
house, which at the time he built it was the only
one on the hill. Still, he managed to squeeze five
bedrooms onto the top floor. There was also a
caretaker's apartment, which has been integrated
into the back of the house.

Outside, terraced gardens make the house
feel secluded, with spectacular views of the

opposite The circular entryway's door is framed by two halves of an octagonal table original to the house. I always place fresh fruit here on a ceramic stand, which is easily picked up en route to the pool or to one of the terraces.

above From the front door, there is a spectacular view of the valley. To arrive at the main entrance, you need to walk up a few stone stairs on the side of the terrace. Provençal pots from the 1940s create a barrier that leads you up the stairs.

left A clock from my grandmother's home in Normandy is displayed on the other half of the octagonal table. It is made of resin and has a distinctive chime.

Mediterranean from nearly every vantage point. Also intact is the ingenious entry system that Anne-Marie's grandmother, Monique Manchez Midy, later devised (in 1934 she married Marcel's son, Robert Midy, Anne-Marie's grandfather). Upon arrival at Lou Miedjou, you are greeted with a shout of "*Salut!*" from the loggia high above the cobbled street. Down comes an electric winch with a grappling hook. This is used to haul up luggage and bags of groceries, so that you don't have to carry anything when you climb the many irregular stone steps that ascend to the house.

When we visit the villa, we love to look through the old family photo albums. There are poignant images from 1939 of Anne-Marie's grandfather and uncle in their military uniforms. During World War II, Marcel was a member of the French army's elite Chasseurs Alpins, or mountain infantry. There are also pictures of her father, Antoine Midy, as a soldier serving on the Tunisian frontier during the Algerian War of the 1950s and '60s.

Anne-Marie was very close to her late grandmother, a renowned Parisian beauty. She was a remarkable woman—an accomplished artist and skier who was active in the French Resistance. One family legend describes how Monique berated a German officer for allowing his troops to use her son's pedal car for their target practice. I can only imagine what a respite sunny Lou Miedjou offered to the Midy family after so many tumultuous wars.

Besides snapshots of the family, the album includes several photographs of the house and its surroundings. There are views of the valley,

opposite I keep our fragile Vallauris Provençal green dishware in the living room behind carved-wooden double doors. It's an ingenious architectural trick because visually it makes you think that another room lies behind, when in fact it is simply a cupboard.

above As much as I've tried to respect the home's original layout, I found it necessary to update a few elements to better accommodate our contemporary lifestyle. To create more space in the living room I moved the dining table into the entrance. The vintage photograph on page 154 shows the original room's configuration. This new arrangement works well. We now have a dining room with the curvilinear plaster staircase as a theatrical backdrop. When the table is not set up for meals, it is used for games. The seat cushions are in needlepoint created by a friend of my grandmother. Above the table is an engraving of Saint Paul, who greets you when you enter the house.

then a bucolic vista of orange and olive groves that were later paved over to make way for supermarkets and car dealerships. The villa's furnishings, Provençal in style, are clearly documented, though the upholstery has changed over the years. The home's cabinets and shelves contain many local artisanal objects: ceramic tableware from Vallauris, blown glass from Biot, and a myriad of woven baskets. The drawers are a treasure trove of antique linens and silverware, which gives Anne-Marie special pleasure each time she sets the table. We did not need to buy any furniture for the house but could not resist adding some Casamidy designs, such as our "Hacienda" headboards and a "Collier" console, perhaps in an effort to create our own personal connection to the past. The furnishings are still mostly as her grandmother left them.

Anne-Marie's grandmother applied her trained visual eye to decorating the house. The color palette was largely drawn from her garden, creating a seamless connection between the interior and exterior spaces. She selected distinctive colors and applied them to the walls in a matte finish so as not to overwhelm the intimate rooms. For example, the master bedroom is painted a subtle green—not too blue and not too yellow. The adjacent blue and pink bedrooms are also calm and inviting.

In 2008, after their father passed away, Anne-Marie and her brother, Emmanuel, inherited the villa. The gift came with some serious complications. While the house looked fine on the surface, upon closer inspection they discovered rotting woodwork, leaks, and other structural problems. Tree roots had grown and damaged the home's plumbing. Tourists eager to take photographs of the village would climb

on the home's roof and damage the tiles. Some of the home's walls were in danger of collapse; the house literally was at risk of sliding down the steep hillside.

Anne-Marie and her brother questioned whether the expense to restore and maintain the house made sense. In the end, they realized that this very special property was so intertwined with their family history that they could not part with it. They focused their efforts on bringing the structure back to its original appearance. The home's walls were rebuilt and reinforced with a core of rebar. In 2012, following a spring of torrential rains, three of the garden's retaining walls collapsed. Sadly, the rosebushes planted by Anne-Marie's great-grandmother and an ancient flowering jasmine vine had to be sacrificed for their reconstruction.

During the renovation, the caretaker's apartment was incorporated into the main house, allowing for an additional bedroom and a television room. Anne-Marie also decided to move the dining table, which was previously located in the living room, into the entry hall of the villa next to the staircase. With these changes, the living room—which previously housed both a television and the table—was freed up to become a more traditional sitting room.

In the South of France, the summer can be very hot. When we spend time in Saint-Paul, we relax by the pool, which was added by Anne-Marie's grandmother in the early 1980s. My brother-in-law and I at last talked Anne-Marie into adding a barbecue on the terrace. She managed to hide it inside a stone wall. We now enjoy lunches in the garden, especially since there is also a new outdoor sink and storage area, which is easier than ferrying dishes up the staircase to the kitchen.

Lou Miedjou has been enjoyed by five generations of Midys. Dinners on the stone terrace can last until two in the morning. We consider ourselves very fortunate that our boys can walk up the worn stone steps and enjoy the views of Saint-Paul-de-Vence, just as their great-great-grandfather Marcel Midy did nearly a century ago. We always love to visit the nearby Maeght Foundation, where the café is furnished entirely in pieces by Diego Giacometti—the very designer who inspired us to create Casamidy.

Anne-Marie spent nearly every summer here throughout her childhood and early teens. After her grandmother passed away, she and her dad spent many summers here as well. More than anything, she remembers the Proustian scents of place: the perfume of orange trees in full bloom, the delicious aroma of lunch on the terrace, the earthy odor of stone floor tiles damp from August rains. To fully understand Anne-Marie as a designer is to witness her in this setting, surrounded by the family furniture and artisanal pieces handpicked by her grandmother. Her favorite touch: a massive wrought-iron key with a hammered heart detail that opens the entry doors to Lou Miedjou.

This passageway leads from the dining area to the kitchen and the living room. Instead of leaving it plain, I added a chair, which comes in handy for an extra guest or as a surface to set a spare set of dishes when I'm serving dinner. Hanging on the wall is a silhouette of a male head by local artist Jean-Charles Blais.

The living room's fireplace is quite
tall because it was originally used
for roasting game and heating up
food. Today we enjoy a fire on chilly
nights and toss in some dried lavender for a heavenly scent. A collection
of ceramics bought at a local market
is displayed on its large mantel. A
set of French doors opens onto the
loggia. I leave them open during
the summer for the breeze. The
Louis XVI bergères used to be in my
mother's Paris apartment. Here at
Lou Miedjou they are refreshed with
red-and-white fabric chosen by my
stepmother, Sophie. I love the way
you can move furnishings into a new
environment simply by changing the
covers. When I'm having guests, I'll
use the English tea table and marble
coffee table for serving drinks
and aperitifs. A light wash of green
paint that has been applied to the
red ceiling beams—original to
the house—enhances their texture.
The door trim has been painted
in a contrasting shade of green.

Midy Minuit umbraf

opposite An eighteenth-century painted box has been placed on our "Collier" console table. Above it is an artisanal manger with wax figures. Both the manger and the sconce were integrated into the wall as part of the original design of the house. To brighten up two antique chairs with threadbare upholstery, I had a pair of slipcovers made with grosgrain detailing.

above, clockwise from top left The sofa sits in a niche with a bookshelf built into one side. It's one of my favorite reading spots. The pillows are made from old embroidered bedcovers. Two (one pictured here) tin gold-leaf suns, original to the house, are placed above a matching set of paneled doors. Beneath them, the Provençal quotes *"midy minuit umbraf"* (noon, midnight, shadow) and *"miedjou ef ma glorio"* (glorious noon) were hand-painted in a loose script. A tall red lamp sits on a prayer stool. The wooden panel to the right leads to the entry hall/dining area. The shelves next to the fireplace showcase old legal tomes, a pharmacy jar, a bronze olive tree, and a ceramic owl from my grandmother's owl collection.

above My father created a large outdoor dining table by placing a glass surface on top of an old unused well. When in bloom, the bougainvillea provides not only a dash of color but also much-needed shade.

right A photo of my grandparents as newlyweds enjoying an outdoor breakfast.

opposite A view of the stone terrace from the top floor. Unfortunately the lovely white flowering oleander tree has not survived.

At Lou Miedjou, each bedroom is referred to by its color. This master bedroom, which is virtually round, is known as the green room. A model jeep serves as a desktop paperweight, and the old transistor radio still works. We no longer use the fireplace. Instead, it holds a straw basket filled with flowers or fresh lavender.

above, clockwise from top left A cheerful pillow continues the house's sun motif. I like the mix of old and new throughout the bedrooms. For example, I placed this old-fashioned miniature green chair near a mixed-media painting of a figure in cobalt blue. Similarly, a bureau covered in English chintz (seen on pages 164–165) resides in the same room opposite a colorful abstract clay fish sculpture.

opposite An eighteenth-century medallion in papier-mâché depicts Marie-Antoinette. (We also have one that shows Louis XVI.) These decorative plaques were made to commemorate the royal wedding.

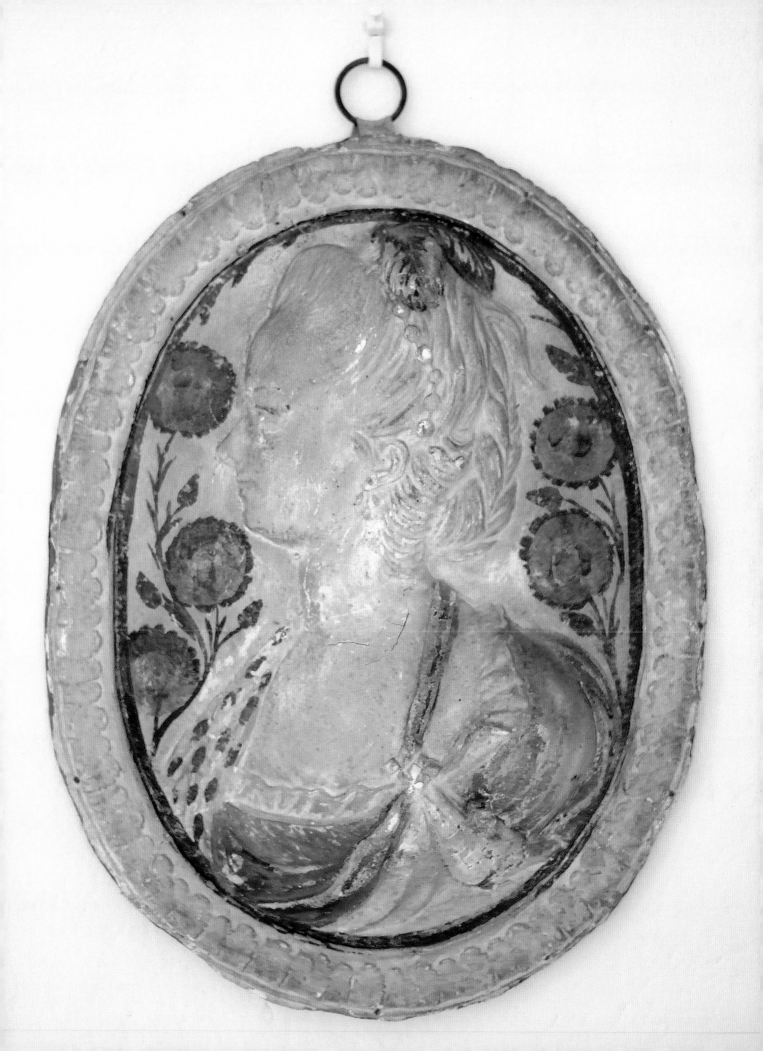

Outside the blue and pink bedrooms, a terrace has a view of Chapelle Saint-Charles-Saint-Claude. A Fermob lounge chair (not pictured) and copper-plated Casamidy side tables live outside. We bring desk chairs here for more seating.

Our "Hacienda" headboard in silver leaf is used in the blue bedroom. In the corner are two small plaster shelves for a light and a glass of water. The entire room is outlined in a dark rose pink, and the black baseboard with flecks of pink and blue sets off the original tiled floor. The female bust and vase are souvenirs from Italy.

opposite I like the simplicity of the long hallway that leads to the guest bedrooms. The black wood mirror with a tin appliqué, purchased in Brussels, provides the passageway's focal point.

above Details of the pink bedroom—a mirror adorns the plaster fireplace (left). Hung above the writing desk is a collection of drawings and watercolors of the town (right).

A white bedroom is furnished
with twin beds—perfect for the
boys' sleepovers. The headboards
are covered in wool-embroidered
linen and are original to the house.
The bedding is Provençal.

opposite Saint-Paul-de-Vence has always been known for its cultural life. Many artists, some legendary, have lived here. Sculptures have been placed around the property, including this marble piece by Manfredo Borsi, which is on the path to the pool area.

above I remember when my father found this bronze donkey, by François-Xavier Lalanne, and had it lifted by crane to the terrace, which was an amazing sight. The trunks that it carries open up to reveal a desk on one side and a bar on the other. The latter is fully functional —we use it often. Our children love to climb on the sculpture.

above The plaster bedroom tower is visible from the bottom terrace, where the pool and pool house are located. The *terrain de pétanque* (pétanque court) is located directly above the pool area (right). To the left of the pool house is a small shady seating area with an old iron bed that was found in a bazaar. Two bronze tables by Louis Cane have been set in front of the daybed. I enjoy the play of the black mosaic circles in the pool with the bronze mask on the wall. A sink, built in the shape of a small town fountain, is at the far side (left).

above The pool was added to the property by my grandmother in the late 1980s. Even though the beach is only a fifteen-minute drive from the house, it can get very hot and crowded. The pool is our oasis—so close to the town, yet so private. Casual sun beds covered in Sunbrella fabric surround the pool. A fig tree on the pathway leading to the pool emits a pleasant smell.

The neighbor's roof tiles have over time pierced through the back wall of the pool area. My grandmother brought the columns from Italy to frame the niche, which she decorated with Italian tile. At the end of the day, when all is tranquil and the air has cooled down, the pool becomes a reflective mirror, lit by our "Symi" lanterns.

above Peering up from the street, one can see
the loggia and the indispensable electric winch, which
is used for hauling up luggage and bags. The loggia's
walls are framed by cement molding and the ceiling
is painted in a sky-blue hue.

above, clockwise from top left When in town, we use this jeep for our adventures. The loggia's curtains get a lot of abuse from wind, rain, and sun. I purchase inexpensive store-bought ones so they can be replaced every season. Seating is incorporated into the plaster-and-stone loggia. The name of the house is carved into the stone wall and has been painted in the same oxblood red as the understated front entrance door.

SONORA

JAMO
A Mexican Ranch

Shortly after my father passed away in 2012, I visited a family friend, Alejandra Redo, in Mexico City. Though we are not blood relatives, the Redos and Almadas are both from the Mexican state of Sinaloa and our families have known each other for nearly six generations. When I was a child, the two families had adjacent ranches in the Sierra Madre mountains of northern Sonora. We remain very close and I have always called Alejandra my *tia* (aunt).

With the loss of my father, I felt a strong sense of longing to return to Sonora, where we had spent part of my childhood. Alejandra kindly offered to let us build a small house on her ranch. I jumped at this opportunity, which seemed like an ideal way to honor the memory of my father while allowing my sons to share the same experience of life on a ranch.

Anne-Marie and I have always been attracted to old buildings and, as a result, we had never before built a house from scratch. Our idea was to create a simple family retreat that we would visit during year-end holidays and in the summer. The terrain that Alejandra had selected for us had no infrastructure apart from a small well located down a hill. We sited the house along a ridge facing southeast in order to take advantage of the best views. The house is oriented toward where the sun rises so that the rooms warm up throughout the day. In designing the house, we took inspiration from

preceding spread A view of the road leading to the ranch's entrance with the property's wooden gates and the mountains in the distance.

opposite The ranch has a herd of more than one hundred buffalo. When horseback riding on the property, we sometimes discover parched bones. Our find of an intact skull is hung on an exterior wall of our house.

following spread The front porch is a place to relax and take in the views of the Ajo Mountains. The wood chair with a sling-back leather seat was a gift to Jorge's dad from Diego Redo, the founder of the ranch. Four matching columns carved in the state of Michoacán hold up the overhang.

opposite The sitting area of the great room includes our "Venice" settee with a tufted back. The pillows are covered in a graphic black-and-white stripe fabric from Toile de Soleil. On the coffee table is a large *maque* (hand-burnished gourd) given to us by Peruvian friends, pétanque balls, and a carved-wood water spigot, which we use to hold odds and ends.

above A pair of Michael Van Buren chairs was refurbished with leather straps (left). The iron fireplace heats up the room almost instantly. We call it the "locomotive" (right).

the classic Flemish farmhouse. Living in Belgium, we had grown enamored of their storybook-like appearance, with their pitched roofs, double-hung windows, and brick walls. We designed a single-story, 1,650-square-foot structure that incorporated many of these elements.

The construction crew we hired to build it were local *vaqueros* (cowboys). With this sort of rustic project, we weren't aiming for perfection. We didn't mind if the cement floor had a few cracks or the brick walls were slightly uneven or the terra-cotta tile on the roof was laid slightly off-kilter. The exterior is white stucco with a long veranda and massive wooden columns encircled

by carved spiraling leaves. We painted the inside of the house in white, and the door-frames and ceiling beams in green. The home was given the name "Jamo," an acronym for Jorge, Anne-Marie and Antoine, and Olivier. We liked how it also sounded like "*J'aime.*"

Jamo is designed around a large central gallery with rafters. On one side is a veranda that, in typical ranch fashion, serves as an outdoor living room on balmy evenings. This is flanked by a second wing, which contains the kitchen, a bathroom, and a guest room. The master bedroom is also located downstairs; above it is the sleeping loft we created for the

above An Uriarte ceramic plate monogrammed with Jorge's family cattle brand was designed by his grandfather.

opposite Our "Grenadier" chairs surround the "Symi" trestle table. Even though the house has a generator, we enjoy eating dinner by the soft glow emitted by glass oil lamps—it feels like a trip back in time.

left to right A rustic Oaxacan chair serves as an extra kitchen surface. Next to it is a sabino wood table from San Miguel. Mexican Cicsa enamelware, typically used on ranches, is displayed on a shelf above the table. A series of oil paintings depicting ranch life hangs in the kitchen. The red door is from Oaxaca. One of my favorite pieces of kitchen equipment is this egg carousel. It is set among other utilitarian Mexican objects, including cactus-fiber brushes for washing dishes and a pressed glass water jar. The kitchen island—a folding cantina (enamel Tecate table)—has a smooth surface that is perfect for making flour tortillas. The kitchen sink is hand-hammered copper. This attractive material was chosen since the sink is visible from the living area.

above Since the guest room is small, we hung a few of our mirrors on the wall in a pattern resembling puzzle pieces; the reflections help to give depth to the small room (left). On a ranch you never have enough hat or coat hooks. This antique hall tree was bought in Nogales by Jorge's dad and has handy hooks and a seat that opens up for storage (right).

above The focal point of our bedroom is this turn-of-the-century cast-iron American Round Oak chimney.

boys, which was inspired by the haylofts in Flemish barns. Antoine and Olivier scamper up a ladder into a private space that feels like a tree house. Perhaps one day we will exchange the ladder for a metal spiral staircase.

To deepen the sense that the house was made by hand, we commissioned architectural elements from some of the artisans we work with at Casamidy. Our metalsmiths crafted wrought-iron window surrounds and doorframes to resemble oak branches. The loft's trestles were milled and painted in our San Miguel de Allende workshop. The carved columns for the veranda come from Michoacán in southwestern Mexico.

We furnished the house with family heirlooms, antiques, as well as willow furniture that we purchased on the side of the road from Yaqui artisans near Ciudad Obregón, Sonora's second-largest city. We often create furniture inspired by our latest interior design project. The ranch inspired a new line of saddle-leather dining chairs that we call the "Grenadier," after the Grenadier Guards in the British army. Saddle leather, which takes on a wonderful luster with wear, is one of my favorite materials. I like to imagine how the chairs will look twenty years from now, after numerous evenings spent here with family and friends.

The kitchen, which is located off the living area, has extra-large windows and doors because it serves a dual purpose: it is not only a cooking space but also serves as a garage for motorcycles and the house's generator when we are not living there. We had originally designed a large pantry but later converted it into a cozy guest room when we realized that my mother needed a place to sleep when visiting her grandkids.

In the middle of the wilderness, conserving energy is paramount. To that end, we created a

above A collection of English hunting prints is hung informally; a dart board, a charro belt, and an architectural drawing fill out the wall composition. Against this wall is a horsehair trunk—a makeshift bar—where bottles of tequila and wine are stored for festive occasions.

opposite A railing of iron and wood was added to the mezzanine. Its design mimics the ranch fencing on the property. Draped over it is a 1940s Saltillo serape that we brought from Brussels. In front is a pair of Michoacán painted children's chairs. Hanging from the beams is a leather-strapped "Hospicio" pendant.

following spread The ranch has remnants of Apache settlements. We asked the boys to paint these tributes to the Apaches. "Prince" and "Indian" mirrors hang above the "Altamura" beds. An Olinalá cedar box has been placed on the "Hunting" dresser, which serves as a night table.

above Since our family shares the bathroom, we each have our own towel hook personalized with our first initial. The wool rug is from San Miguel and woven into it is Jorge's family's ranch brand design (left). Above the single sink hangs a "Hiver" mirror in iron. To break up the warm copper/wood tonalities of the bathroom, we chose this turquoise Oaxacan door (right).

opposite The hand-hammered copper bathtub has a jewel-like quality, especially when we light the candles in the candelabra, which came from a church. The material seemed apt since Sonora has a tradition of copper mining.

opposite A lot of wood is needed to heat up the house. We store it in this painted iron rack. The boys use their wagon to help bring the logs inside.

clockwise from bottom left We love the ranch's functional features, like the water troughs and corral. In our home, this boot shelf keeps our footwear off the ground and away from creepy-crawlies and playful dogs. We saddle up for riding adventures and the ranch dogs come along.

massive metal chimney (our ironsmith baptized it the "locomotive") attached to a wood-burning stove that efficiently heats the living area. The ranch has many oak trees, some of which were felled by lightning, and so we have plenty of kindling. The kitchen, including the refrigerator, runs on gas. We have jerry cans that we fill up every time we go into town. Because the house is way off the grid, we use a small generator that we turn on at dusk and off after dinner. It allows everyone to charge up his or her electronics. We usually watch a movie and fall asleep by eleven o'clock at night.

Jamo is an intimate place. Everyone participates in chores, such as bringing in firewood for the stoves and fireplace. But while there is work to be done, there are also countless pleasures—from sunset horseback rides to moonlit walks under the bright stars. During the day, we picnic in the nearby mountains, and it has become a tradition to play pétanque before dinner (albeit in cowboy boots instead of espadrilles). In this rustic and informal setting, our boys have the freedom to explore and enjoy nature, just as Alejandra and I did when we were kids.

above and opposite At night, around a bonfire, we talk about the day's adventures. The porch is illuminated with oil lamps and Christmas lights.

PART THREE

CASAMIDY

OUR DESIGN PROCESS

Anne-Marie and I both value traditional craftsmanship and we share a design sensibility. But one reason our Casamidy partnership works is that we give each other plenty of creative autonomy as designers. Each piece in our collection is designed either by Anne-Marie or me. We rarely collaborate directly on designs, but of course we are greatly influenced by each other's work.

I am inspired by the idea of furniture that enhances with wear. My three favorite materials are saddle leather, wrought iron, and oak. Since I worked in home furnishing shops while in college, I have a tendency to think like a salesperson: I am conscious of price points and such practical matters as functionality.

Anne-Marie takes a free-spirited, artistic approach to her work. I remember when she first described her idea to me of a line of furniture that "flowed in the wind." One day I found her in the Casamidy studio with Sergio and Ricardo painstakingly assembling long chains out of tiny hand-cut pieces of tin that had been gilded with silver on one side and gold on the other. I admit I was skeptical when I saw the complexity of assembling the chains, which were to hang from wrought-iron bases. The line (Anne-Marie named it "Collier," like a necklace) turned out to be well received. The results have an almost Byzantine-like quality and, sure enough, if you leave a door or window open, the shimmering links will rustle and move in the breeze.

As designers, we are constantly searching for new ideas. Sometimes a new design, like the "Collier," is based on new ways of connecting or

above When we removed layers of paint from the walls of our San Miguel office, we discovered this colorful antique tile work along with some damaged fresco details, which were kept (left). Jorge and I on our beloved Honda 90cc motorcycle, with its reupholstered leather seat. Traveling by motorcycle is the easiest way to get from one workshop to another (right).

preceding spread Alejandro Rodriguez soldering our custom "Branch" console in his San Miguel de Allende workshop.

opposite A pair of "Louis" armchairs as specified by the interior designer Celerie Kemble.

opposite, clockwise from top left Our "Almidi Opium" mirror reflects the cement tile original to the house. A "Bokkusu" daybed with a backdrop of papier-mâché *sonajas* (rattles) and *Días de los Muertos* (Day of the Dead) figurines. The "Manchez" chairs are upholstered in an Otomi embroidered fabric. Our "Molecule" table is displayed in the studio. In the middle of the traditional patio are a fountain and an orange tree. The funky 1950s ceramic steps are used for displaying potted plants.

attaching existing elements or materials. Memories of our childhood homes have also had a great impact on our design practice. We are constantly inspired by life's experiences— by our own evolving tastes, the needs of our children, and our ever-changing surroundings. We have always been attracted to flea market finds for what they can teach us about how earlier generations approached the design of objects.

Travel is also a major influence. We try to create products that relate to our experience of being in different places and absorbing the local artistry. On a recent trip to Venice, we searched for unusual geometric patterns (the city is filled with them, from mosaic tile floors to the designs on centuries-old wooden doors), which we photographed and later adapted into a line of wrought-iron mirror frames for our "Venezia" collection. We named each design after the neighborhood where we found the pattern: Murano, Rialto, Dogana, St. Mark's, and so on. Happenstance also plays a role. On the Venice trip, we rode in a water taxi with a tufted aqua plastic bench. The shape and color inspired our "Venezia" settee.

The work of other designers is a constant source of influence. Our heroes include such twentieth-century furniture design icons as Jacques Adnet, Charlotte Perriand, Karl Aubock, and Diego Giacometti. Another favorite of ours is the Cuban-born designer Clara Porset, who adapted traditional Mexican handicrafts and materials, as well as pre-Columbian art, for designs that were nevertheless completely unique and her own. The Mexican modernist architect Luis Barragán used her furniture in his interiors.

Casamidy's designs are created in close collaboration with many trained artisans. We work with more than thirty blacksmiths alone. Each one of them is a "maestro" with his

own take on the material. Anne-Marie and I are always able to recognize their signature traits. In addition to iron and tinsmiths, we also collaborate with leather and woodworkers, glassblowers, glaziers, upholsterers, mosaic artists, lampshade makers, paint and finish specialists, weavers, and many other types of craftspeople. Frequently, they will offer suggestions that allow us to improve upon our ideas, and show us innovative textures and finishes that they have developed on their own. These relationships have resulted in many new Casamidy collections.

Our studio and showroom is located in the back of a delightful building in San Miguel de Allende that was designed by Zeferino Gutierrez, a local stonemason and architect of the nineteenth-century façade of the town's iconic La Parroquia church. Our building, originally a house, dates from 1880 and retains some of the original brightly colored decorative wall paintings. Casamidy occupies the home's former kitchen, adjacent patio, and a bedroom. We photograph most of our products here as well as outside on the cobblestone street. Each member of the Casamidy studio has a specific task: Arturo Avalos is our primary draftsman, Roberto Hernandez chooses the artisan who will work on each piece and oversees the furniture orders, Gabriel Villafranco does quality control, while Bruno Tellez takes photos when we are away in Brussels.

We're not overly strict about the execution of our designs. We provide drawings with dimensions and then trust that the artisan will use his or her best judgment in resolving the details. By doing so, everyone involved in the creation of a Casamidy piece—from Anne-Marie and me to the craftsmen with whom we collaborate, not to mention the wonderful clients who commission our furniture—can share a mutual sense of pride in the finished product.

THE ARTISANS

Top row, left to right **Gabriel Villafranco**—our production coordinator. **Edouardo Deanda**—makes our graphic mirrors. His son Omar is learning the craft. **Arturo Avalos**—our draftsman. **Miguel Moreno**—produces most of our upholstery and has been with us since the very beginning. *Bottom row, left to right* **Antonio and Salvador Salazar**—two brothers who manufacture most of our lanterns. **Jose-Luis Gutierrez and Juan-Manuel Gonzalez**—oak specialists. **Refugio Rico**—the ironsmith who helps create our prototypes and most complicated pieces. **Cecilio Botes**—a master tinsmith.

Casamidy relies on close working relationships with many skilled artisans.

Top row, left to right **Rosario Cervantes**—learned the upholstery trade from her father and now assists him with upholstery production. **Monica Cacho**—with her assistant, ensures safe delivery of Casamidy pieces. **Pedro Lozada**—a glazier. **Sandra Sanchez**—with members of her family, embroiders the Otomi textiles that we employ. *Bottom row, left to right* **Sergio Chavez**—produces some of our metallic finishes. **Ernesto Hernandez**—the soul behind our leather designs. **Rosa Vasquez**—keeps our busy office clean. **Veronica Rios and Juan-Carlos Espinoza**—in charge of installing the glass panels in our lanterns.

Top row, left to right **Bruno Tellez**—our senior production manager and photographer. **Fernanda Zapian and Karina Arratia**—handle our international shipments. **Luis-Enrique Pastor with his assistant Luis-Gerado Vasquez**—especially adept with raw iron textures. **Alberto Morin**—constructs our "Molecular" bases. *Bottom row, left to right* **Alejandro Gonzalez**—responsible for our "Varenne" line. **Teodulo Rodriguez**—a straw weaver. **Rosalio Vilchis with his son Josser-Armando and assistant Gustavo Ramos**—a master woodworker specializing in such elaborate pieces as our "Symi" trestle table and "Loop" mirrors. **Gerardo Perez**—our powder coater.

Top row, left to right **Ricardo Banda**—a tinsmith extraordinaire who spends countless hours on our "Collier" pieces. **Jorge and Alejandro Gomez**—in charge of lacquering our raw metal pieces. **Roberto Hernandez**— our manager, who makes everything come together. **Martin Gonzalez and Yahir Martin**—our "Hacienda" headboard specialists. *Bottom row, left to right* **Juan Gonzalez**—an ironsmith. **Lander Rodriguez**—the sounding board for Casamidy's website. **Miguel-Angel Grimaldo and Gilberto Gutierrez**—our electroplate specialists. **Alberto Lopez**—excels in custom-color matching.

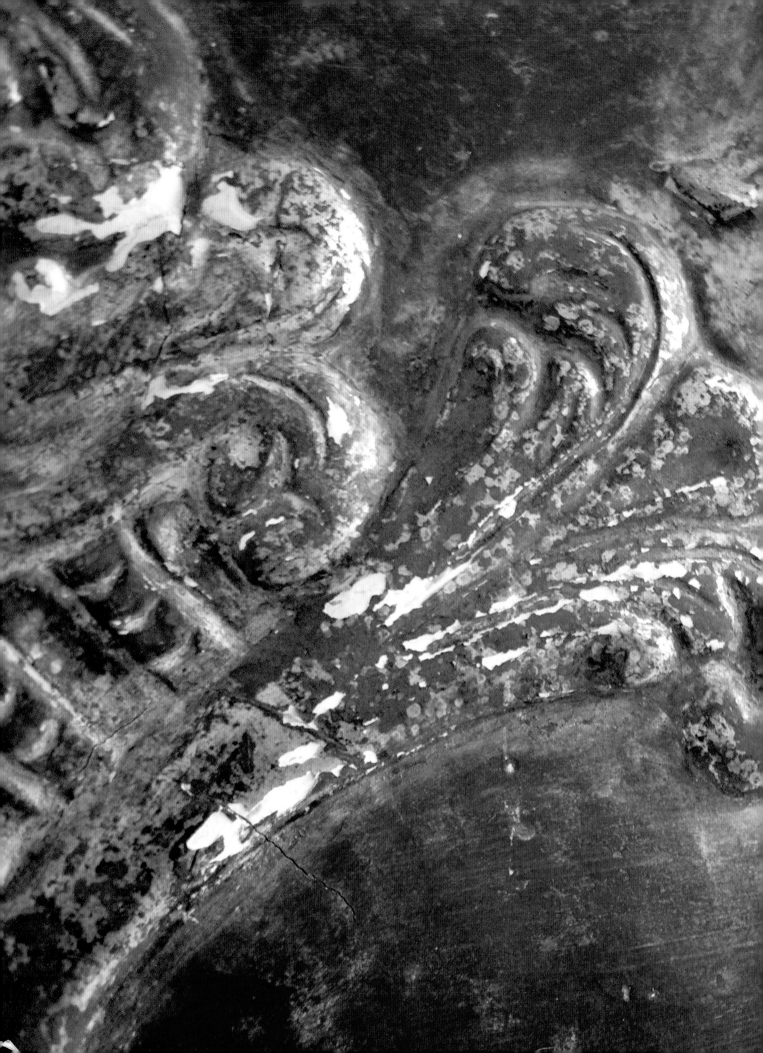

OUR ADDRESS BOOK

A list of resources referenced in *The Artisanal Home*
that share a commitment to the handmade.

Belgium

Grande Droguerie Le Lion
Restoration products
Rue de Laeken 55
1000 Brussels
+32 (0) 2 217 42 02
www.le-lion.be

K. Loan
Vintage furnishings
Rue Blaes 101
1000 Brussels
+32 (0) 2 502 56 19
www.kloan.be

La Savonnerie
Vintage furnishings
Rue Emile Bouilliot 20
1050 Brussels
+32 (0) 2 346 30 87

Le Typographe
Letterpress stationery
Rue Americaine 67
1050 Brussels
+32 (0) 2 345 16 76
www.typographe.be

Percaline
Interior design services
including upholstery
Rue Africaine 98
1060 Saint-Gilles
+32 (0) 2 537 68 70

Scénes de Ménages
Vintage furnishings
Place Brugmann 4
1050 Brussels
+32 (0) 2 344 32 95

Weekend Antiques Market
Petit Sablon Square
1000 Brussels

France

BHV (Bazar de l'Hôtel de Ville)
Housewares and a wonderful
hardware selection
52 Rue de Rivoli
75189 Paris
+33 (9) 77 40 14 00
www.bhv.fr

Carrelages des Suds
Tiles
24 Boulevard Saint-Germain
75005 Paris
+33 (1) 40 51 01 01

Caravane
Pillows, furniture, and rugs
6 Rue Pavée
75004 Paris
France
+33 (1) 44 61 04 20
www.caravane.fr

Fermob
Outdoor furniture
Parc Actival
01140 Thoissey
+33 (0) 4 74 04 97 93
www.fermob.fr

Jérôme Lepert
Industrial furniture
106 Rue Vieille du Temple
75003 Paris
+33 (0) 6 10 18 18 88

La Boutique de Léa
Provençal tablecloths and placemats
Espace Sainte-Claire
06570 Saint-Paul-de-Vence
+33 (0) 4 93 32 68 05

La Collégiale
Provençal fabrics and
artisanal crafts
Rond Point Sainte-Claire
06570 Saint-Paul-de-Vence
+33 (0) 4 93 32 80 94

La Quincaillerie
Hardware
3 and 4 Boulevard Saint-Germain
75005 Paris
+33 (1) 46 33 66 71
www.laquincaillerie.com

Couleurs du Temps
Rugs and home accessories
1119 Route de la Colle
06570 Saint-Paul-de-Vence
+33 (0) 4 93 32 91 50
www.couleursdutemps.fr

Mushkane
Felt rugs
3 Rue Pastourelle
75003 Paris
+33 (0) 9 77 06 53 47
www.muskhane.fr

Sentou
Colorful contemporary designs
29 Rue François Miron
75004 Paris
+33 (0) 1 42 78 50 60
www.sentou.fr

Société des Chaînes du Marais
Chains for chandeliers
and other uses
20 Rue Charlot
75003 Paris
France
+33 (1) 42 72 71 34

Mexico

Atelier Stellis
Stone mosaic designs
Fabrica de la Aurora
Calzada de la Aurora
San Miguel de Allende
Guanajuato 37700
+52 (415) 154-4202
www.atelierstellis.com

Bazar Arte Viejo
Bazaar
Hidalgo 17
San Miguel de Allende
Guanajuato 37700
+52 (415) 154-3013
bazar_arte_viejo@hotmail.com

Casa Katalina
Flower candles
Jesús 26
San Miguel de Allende
Guanajuato 37700
+52 (415) 150-0061
katherineleutzinger@gmail.com

Casa Maxwell
Ceramics
Canal 14
Colonia Centro
San Miguel de Allende
Guanajuato 37700
+52 (415) 152-0247
www.maxwell.freeservers.com

Casa Michoacana
Mexican artisanal objects
Calzada de la Aurora 23
San Miguel de Allende
Guanajuato 37700
+52 (415) 154-5008

Ceramica Antique
Tiles
Fábrica de la Aurora
San Miguel de Allende
Guanajuato 37700
+52 (415) 154-9629
www.ceramicaantique.com

Cinsa Sa de Cv
Enamelware and oil lamps
Boulevard Isidro Lopez Zertuche 1495
Saltillo Centro, Coahuila 25000
+52 (844) 411-6000
www.cinsa.com.mx

Colors
Mexican folk art and kitschy objects
Zacateros 48
San Miguel de Allende
Guanajuato 37700
+52 (415) 152-3070
www.colorssanmiguel.com

overleaf A detail of my grandmother's Italian Baroque bed.

Counter Cultures
Bathroom accessories, including
copper bathtubs and sinks
Zacateros 21
San Miguel de Allende
Guanajuato 37700
+52 (415) 154-8375
www.counter-cultures.com

Galeria Atotonilco
Mexican artisanal objects
(by appointment only)
+52 (415) 185-2225
U.S. and Canada +1 (510) 295-4097
www.folkartsanmiguel.com

Insh'ala
Rugs and decorative objects
Aldama 30
Colonia Centro
San Miguel de Allende
Guanajuato 37700
+52 (415) 152-8355
U.S. +1 (303) 877-9814
www.inshalaimports.com

La Misión
Bazaar
Calzada de le Aurora 7
San Miguel de Allende
Guanajuato 37700
+52 (415) 122-3924
ant_mexsma@hotmail.com

Mi Casa Es Tu
Chiapas pillows
Calle Diez de Sollano 27
San Miguel de Allende
Guanajuato 37700
+52 (415) 152-3758
www.kiri.com.mx

Mixta
Eclectic furnishings
Pila Seca 3
San Miguel de Allende
Guanajuato 37700
+52 (415) 152-7343
www.mixtasanmiguel.com

Otomi Fabric
Fabrics
Mercado de Artesania
Plaza Lanatón
San Miguel de Allende
Guanajuato 37700

Talavera Cortes Sa de Cv
Mexican tiles
Distrito Federal 8
37800 Dolores Hidalgo
Guanajuato
+52 (418) 182-0900
www.talaveracortes.com.mx

Uriarte
Classic Talavera dishware
4 Poniente 911
Colonia Centro
Puebla 72000
+52 (222) 232-1598
www.uriartetalavera.com.mx

United States

Acacia Art & Antiques
Ranch accessories
69 Main Street
Bisbee, Arizona 85603
+1 (520) 432-2752
www.acacia-bisbee.com

Duralee
Fabrics
+1 (800) 275-3872
www.duralee.com

Filson
Blankets
+1 (800) 624-0201
www.filson.com

Jim Thompson Fabrics
Fabrics
D&D Building, #502
979 Third Avenue
New York, NY 10022
+1 (212) 546-9001
www.jimthompsonfabrics.com

Les Toiles Du Soleil
Fabrics
261 West 19th Street
New York, NY 10011
United States
+1 (212) 229-4730
www.lestoilesdusoleilnyc.com

International

B&B Italia
Furniture
www.bebitalia.com

Cole & Son
Wallpaper
www.cole-and-son.com

Farrow & Ball
Paints
www.farrow-ball.com

Ikea
Rugs
www.ikea.com

Marimekko
Fabrics
www.marimekko.com

Muji
Accessories and furniture
www.muji.com

Sunbrella
Outdoor fabrics
www.sunbrella.com

International Galleries
and Artists

Galerie Catherine Issert
Artists: Anne Pesce, Ben,
and Jean-Charles Blais
2 Route des Serres
06750 Saint-Paul-de-Vence
France
+33 (4) 93 32 96 92
www.galerie-issert.com

Galeria Omr
Artist: Aldo Chaparro
Plaza Rio de Janerio 54
Mexico City
Roma 06700
Mexico
+52 1 (5) 511-1179

Galeria Yam
Artist: Cristobal Gajardo
Ancha de San Antonio 20
San Miguel de Allende
Guanajuato 37700
Mexico
+52 (415) 150-6052
www.yamgallery.com

Paul Kasmin Gallery
Artist: François-Xavier Lalanne
515 West 27th Street
New York, NY 10001
United States
+1 (212) 563-4474
www.paulkasmingallery.com

Amber Eagle
+52 (415) 153-3213
ambereagle@hotmail.com

Bill Killen
+1 (401) 219-1554
www.billkillen.com

Paulo Sartorio Netto
+1 (917) 459-5053
sartorionetto@gmail.com

Susan Plum
+1 (713) 542-6986
www.susanplum.com

Kent Rogowski
+1 (718) 782-4501
www.kentrogowski.com

CREDITS

Jorge Almada—pages 4, 10–12, 14 (top), 22–23, 26–29, 32, 47 (bottom), 112–113, 123 (top), 130, 136 (bottom, left), 178 (left), 183 (top, left), 184–199, 202–209, 212, 214–217, 222, 224

Henry Bourne—pages 114–121

Simon Brown—pages 7, 31, 35–36, 42–43, 48 (left), 49–51

Pieter Estersohn—pages 81–89, 91–95

François Halard—pages 55, 58–59, 66–67, 74–79, 97–111

Ricardo Labougle—pages 52–53, 56–57, 60–65, 68–72, 129, 131–135, 136 (top, right and bottom, right), 140–141, 144, 210 (top, right)

Anne-Marie Midy—pages 2, 8, 19 (bottom), 20–21, 24–25, 48 (right), 122, 123 (bottom, left and right), 124–127, 137, 138–139, 142–143, 145–148, 153 (bottom), 154 (right), 166–167, 183 (bottom, middle), 200–201, 210 (top, left), 218–219, endpaper and jacket (front and back) images

Bruno Tellez—page 211

Simon Upton—pages 33–34, 37, 39–41, 44–46, 47 (top), 150–152, 153 (top, left and right), 155, 157–161, 162 (top), 164–165, 168–177, 178 (right), 179–182, 183 (bottom, left and right)

The painting *Petit Chien Jouant Avec un Soulier* by Dominique Doncre, dated 1785, that appears on page 136 has been reprinted with the permission of the Musée de la Chasse et de la Nature, Paris, France. Photograph © Sylvie Durand

SPECIAL THANKS TO

Ingrid Abramovitch, Sandy Gilbert, Celerie Kemble, Charles Miers, and Anita Sarsidi, who made *The Artisanal Home* happen.

Our studio staff—Arturo Avalos, Roberto Hernandez, Bruno Tellez, and Gabriel Villafranco.

Cina Alexander, Nathalie Aubert, Noemi Bonazzi, Michael Boodro, Nicole Bouyeres, Hamish Bowles, Hatta Byng, Julie Carlson, Carmen Cordera, Marie-Christine Dawance, Delphine Delhostal, Dorsey Gardener, Melanio Gomez, Mieke Ten Have, Jessica Hayns, Susana Laborde, Sarah Luhtala, Michelle Magazine, Marco Martinez, Antoine and Sophie Midy, Eric Pike, Alejandra Redo, Margaret Russell, Regine and François Sicart, Annie Kelly and Tim Street-Porter, Alta Tingle, Marta Turok, Anne-Marie Wilson, Marilyn Younglove, and our clients, who have been especially supportive of Casamidy.

opposite A photograph of the hacienda Jaral de Berrio, which captures the surrealistic quality of Mexico that I fell in love with. A couple of the rooms are without roofs; the local farmers sometimes dry their beans in these open spaces. And sheep will occasionally wander through.

page 2 The living area in our rooftop pied-à-terre
in the Marais's Hôtel d'Hallwyl.

page 4 The focal point of the master bedroom in our
Brussels house is the original marble fireplace. The rug,
a reproduction of a traditional Tibetan tiger design, partially
covers a cut-wool rug. It muffles the noise from the creaky
wooden floor and adds visual interest to the space. The
subtle colors of both rugs contrast with the rich dark floor.
The Empire-style chest and early twentieth-century
French rocking chair are inherited pieces.

First published in the United States of America in 2014
by Rizzoli International Publications, Inc.
300 Park Avenue South
New York, New York 10010
www.rizzoliusa.com

2014 2015 2016 2017 / 10 9 8 7 6 5 4 3 2 1

Printed in China

ISBN 13: 978-0-8478-4366-4

Library of Congress Control Number: 2014942047

Project Editor: Sandra Gilbert
Graphic Design: Anne-Marie Midy